The Nature Process is a personal invitation from Gaia herself to support you at the deepest level possible in order to experience the maximum possible growth. It is an invitation to trust Life in ways you've never imagined. Rather than "anthropomorphizing Earth" Tabitha guides us through an important journey in how we can become more Earth-like. This distinction is critical if we are to fully reconnect, heal, and evolve as a species. The Nature Process is pure genius because it outlines a 'natural process' not dependent on our intellects, experts, or facilitators. Tabitha illuminates how we can all tap into Nature's wisdom and follow where it leads. If you long to go beyond ecological theory and into loving partnership with Nature – as you transform your life – this is the field guide for you.

- TreeSisters
www.treesisters.org

The Nature Process

How to easily and effortlessly step into your natural power and be the change you want to make in the world

By

Tabi(tha) Jayne

Copyright © 2014 Tabitha Jayne Ltd

All rights reserved. No part of this book may be used or reproduced by any means, graphic, electronic, or mechanical, including photocopying, recording, taping or by any information storage retrieval system without the written permission of the author except in the case of brief quotations embodied in critical articles and reviews.

Bulk copies of the book may be ordered by contacting the author direct: tabitha@tabithajayne.com

ISBN-13: 978-1502483355
ISBN-10:1502483351

Because of the dynamic nature of the Internet, any web addresses or links contained in this book may have changed since publication and may no longer be valid. The views expressed in this work are solely those of the author and do not necessarily reflect the views of the publisher, and the publisher hereby disclaims any responsibility for them.

The author of this book does not dispense medical advice or prescribe the use of any technique as a form of treatment for physical, emotional, or medical problems without the advice of a physician, either directly or indirectly. The intent of the author is only to offer information of a general nature to help you in your quest for personal and planetary well-being. In the event you use any of the information in this book for yourself, which is your constitutional right, the author and the publisher assume no responsibility for your actions.

Front Cover Picture © Paul Prescott | Dreamstime

Contents

Introduction 1
Chapter 1: Think Differently About Nature 11
    The Problem With Mother Earth 12
    The Consciousness of Nature 14
    Aristotle's Hierarchy of Nature 16
    Nature Outside Reflects Nature Within 18
    A New Way of Sensing the World 20
    My Journey Back to Nature 22
Chapter 2: The Nature Process 31
    1. Natural Presence 32
    2. Natural Body 33
    3. Natural Attractions 34
    4. Natural Communication 35
    5. Natural Release 36
    The Nature Process In Action 37
Chapter 3: Natural Presence 39
    The Connection Between Meditation and Nature 40
    The Earth's Connection to Our Brain 41
    Connecting to Different Aspects of Nature 43
    The Difference Between Vibration and Frequency 44
    Daniel Kish - Human Echolocation Expert 44
    The Reality of Our Sensory Nature 46
    The Fifty-Four Senses 48
    Radiation Senses 49
    Feeling Senses 50
    Chemical Senses 52
    Mental Senses 53
    Experience Your Fifty-Four Senses 60
    The Vibration of Our Natural Senses 62
    Explore Nature with Your Senses in Both the Country and the City
    63
Chapter 4: Natural Body 67

- How the Body Responds to Stress 68
- How the Mind Affects the Body 69
- Horses: Masters of Body Awareness 70
- How the Body Naturally Releases Energy 72
- Body Awareness Guided Visualization 74
- Connect to Your Natural Body 77
- How to Adapt Your Natural Body to Physical Disability 79
- The Body's Response to Emotions 80
- Connect Your Natural Body to Your Natural Presence 81

Chapter 5: Natural Attractions 83
- The Importance of Following Your Natural Attractions 84
- Learn About Natural Attractions from Cats 86
- Natural Attractions in Working Life 89
- Natural Attraction in Exercise 90
- The Insanity of Civilization 90
- Put Those Heels Away 92
- Forget About The Bra 93
- Natural Attractions and Growth 94
- Find the Blocks in Your Natural Attractions 95
- Connect Your Natural Attractions to Nature 96
- Integrate Natural Attractions Into The Nature Process 98

Chapter 6: Natural Communication 101
- The Gaia Hypothesis 102
- Tilly Smith: Tsunami Heroine 103
- How to Communicate With Nature 105
- Get Permission to Connect to Nature 107
- The Permission Exercise 109
- How to Know You've Gotten Consent 110
- Engaging in Natural Communication 112
- Natural Communication with Animals 114
- Natural Communication with Trees and Plants 115
- Natural Communication with Stones, Stars, and Water 116
- Consolidate Natural Communication Into The Nature Process 117

Chapter 7: Natural Release 119
- Use Your Heart 120
- The Power of Visualization 121
- The Nature Process: A Real-Time Account 122

A Different Perspective on The Nature Process 131
How to Fully Integrate Your Experience into Your Psyche..............133
Some Final Reminders 135
Chapter 8: Get Out of Your Own Way 137
Don't Let Yourself Get Distracted 138
Own Your Emotions...138
Explore Your Beliefs About Nature 140
Don't Buy Into "Green" Marketing 141
Observe Your Language 144
Nature Reflects You 145
Let Your Imagination Run Free 146
Start Asking "What If?" 148
Stay Connected..148
Chapter 9: Be The Change 151
Additional Resources 167
The Nature Process Workshops/Retreats 167
The Nature Process Presentations 167
The Nature Process Facilitator Training 168
The Nature Process Affiliate Scheme 168
About Tabi(tha) Jayne...169
Acknowledgements 170
Pay It Forward 171

Introduction

Our world faces a crisis as yet unperceived by those possessing power to make great decisions for good or evil.

- Albert Einstein

There's something wrong with the world we live in. You've felt it your entire life. At first you didn't know exactly what it was. You couldn't explain it. Yet no matter what's happened in your life it's been there, like a splinter in your mind.

As you've grown up you've watched as the world has started to melt into a hotbed of global crisis. Civilization as we know it is breaking down.

Despite the fear and uncertainty that's currently sweeping the planet, deep down within you is a seed of hope. Hope that the change we're currently experiencing is the birth of something new. Hope that humanity can evolve alongside the planet and repair the damage that we've created. Hope that a better future awaits all of us.

You look around at the way humanity currently lives and know that it doesn't have to be like this.

You're right.

There is another way.

In the new way, business puts the planet before profits.

Leaders put people before power.

Success is measured by how much positive impact you make.

Individually, we let go of the stories that keep us stuck and step into the complete awesomeness of who we are born to be.

Collectively, we bring the impossible into reality. We step beyond the limitations of ego and self.

Peace reigns. Equality exists for all.

The world is whole.

Balanced.

Now I have no idea *how* this will happen, and maybe neither do you.

I only know that it *will*.

Why?

I believe in nature.

The nature around us.

The nature within me and within you.

Together we are one.

And together we're changing the world.

When I forget that we can change the world, I go to back to nature.

I am reminded.

The next step is revealed.

I take action.

I'm helping to re-birth the world.

The time is *now*.

Are you in?

I'm offering you a choice just like Morpheus did with Neo in the *The Matrix*.

You can put down this book, take the blue pill, and continue on with your life as it is. Believe whatever you want.

Or you can take the red pill. Access your forgotten childhood experiences of joy and wonder in nature. Follow the white rabbit into its hole and discover just how deep it connects you to the Earth.

The choice is yours. All that nature is offering you when you consciously connect with it through The Nature Process is the truth. Nothing more. Yet this truth will fundamentally change your life.

It'll alter how you view this world and your role in it. It'll allow you to see just how powerful you truly are; and once you see this, re-birthing the world will be nothing more than a side effect of you stepping into your natural power.

Consciously connecting to nature is like plugging yourself into the most powerful source of energy known to humanity.

It becomes easy and effortless to create the life you want, to let go of the pain of the past and wake up every morning feeling truly alive.

Your relationships with your loved ones will improve. You'll view your life from a powerful and empowering perspective that gives you the courage to take action towards your dreams.

As you do you'll help create the world that we all want to live in.

Deep down you already know this is possible. It's this knowledge that has brought you to this book. It's this knowledge that has led me to write this book.

You see, my childhood was traumatic. Severe ill health. Bullying. Domestic violence. Rape. For peace I turned to books, nature, and magic. Drugs and alcohol masked the pain.

Then, when I was twenty-two, my younger brother Peter died in a car accident.

I had to find a new path.

The next five years were spent trying to turn the worst thing that ever happened to me into the best. I devoted my time and energy to healing, spiritual growth, work, university, and the charity I was inspired to found to help young adults affected by bereavement.

Instead of truly healing, I ended up tired, stressed, and burnt out.

I needed a change. When I saw the opportunity to volunteer in Northern Spain I took it because of my brother Peter's nickname—Pedro. The nature there was amazing: vivid, green and so alive. Inspired by this, I decided to move there.

A couple of years later, at a woman's weekend retreat in rural Galicia, I met an old oak tree at the corner of a field. The power emanating from this tree was incredible. All weekend I felt the tree calling me, not with words, but with a physical pull that kept my awareness returning again and again to the tree.

On the last day I finally climbed the tree, after getting its permission to do so. Through my senses I could feel the tree telling me to climb out to the edge of its branches to remove some trapped plastic, then slide down the branch to the earth. I thought I was freaking mad as I followed the tree's instructions on how to reach the outer branches. Yet the exhilaration I felt from trusting the tree was phenomenal.

As I perched on a swaying branch hidden high amongst the leaves, I felt at peace and fully connected to my brother. I remembered when we'd scattered Peter's ashes in the woodland area, as he'd requested. We'd gone back a few days later to find bright red flowers carpeting the earth where his ashes had fallen.

It hit me. Nature and my brother were one. Peter was everywhere. I hadn't lost my brother. He was still here. Like magic, with a click of my fingers, the pain melted away to be replaced by the most immense feeling of love and connection that remains with me to this day.

That's the power of nature.

I started applying this to every area of my life. The deeper I connected with nature, the deeper I connected with myself. Blocks and limiting beliefs that had been with me for years melted away in the face of consciously connecting to nature.

Yet there was one area of my life to which I had never thought to apply this connection with nature. That was my business. In December 2013, nature challenged me to bring it fully into my business. The following months were incredible.

In just nine months, my email list went from 98 people to 1,202 people.

With a few ups and downs, my business revenue steadily climbed: Zero in December 2013, $98 in January 2014, and two dollars in February. Then up to $2,579 in March, $5,000 in April, and $9,600 in May.

I redesigned my whole website. Myself. In two days. If you include the time it took to write the copy, then make it two weeks.

In March, my coach at the time challenged me to take the work I did with people individually and develop it into a process. This is the result: The Nature Process, first the online program and now the book.

On May 15th 2014, I held a free webinar to promote The Nature Process. I had 380 sign-ups and 77 people attended live, eight of whom signed up for the program immediately.

In total, 77 people from twelve countries signed up to go through The Nature Process.

What was totally cool is that this program gave me a chance to walk my talk. I believe that businesses need to put the planet before profits. To model this, I gave 100% of the profits from The Nature Process to a non-profit organization called TreeSisters, which supports both emerging feminine leadership and reforestation of the planet—two things that can save humanity from self-destruction.

I didn't put a lot of effort or marketing to get these results. In fact, I spent most of those six months consciously connecting with nature, sleeping, reading trashy erotica, and travelling, mostly to visit family and friends.

My personal budget was $575 per month, which came from another source. Now this might trigger your money and business beliefs; after all, what about profit?

The Nature Process comes from nature itself. I am merely the messenger. I did this deliberately so that I could create a revolutionary business model that puts planet first, not profit.

That's the power of nature.

Since then I've stopped taking on new one-to-one clients and focused on creating a group program that supports people truly interested in creating personal and planetary transformation and growth. My business revenue went down as I consciously earned no income in June and July, instead putting all my energy into preparing the group program.

By the time I launched this program in August 2014, I had earned nearly $9,000 from people signing up. I have a small group of wonderful people all using the Tree of Transformation to create quantum leaps in their life, as well as people registered to be trained in The Nature Process.

I was living on Ibiza, an island in the Mediterranean Sea, seventy-nine kilometers (forty-nine miles) off the coast of the city of Valencia, in eastern Spain. It is the third largest of the Balearic Islands, an autonomous community of Spain. In June I left Ibiza and went back to Scotland to spend some weeks with family before I headed out to France. I spent a month there with family and friends, writing this book and preparing for the group program.

Then I returned to Scotland, via Andorra and Barcelona, before heading back out to Ibiza via New York and London. Once in Ibiza I'll be developing and launching some more group programs before returning back to Scotland in time for Christmas and two of my nieces' birthdays in January.

That's the power of nature: The freedom to live your life in the way you want, trusting that you'll be supported every step of the way.

While I wanted to give you some background about my journey, this book is not about my story and business results from consciously connecting to nature. It's about you and your future.

To paraphrase John Lennon, some might say that you're a dreamer. You're naturally drawn to find the positive in any situation, even when life gives you lemons.

You've always had an appreciation for nature, which hasn't necessarily been shared by those around you. You've struggled to put this into words. Just like you've struggled with various life challenges.

You've had certain experiences that have challenged how you view both yourself and the world. These experiences have forced you to confront your fears and deal with your worst nightmares.

Yet despite doing this, you know that you're not yet fully healed. You're not living life as fully as you know you could. You still have dreams left unfulfilled. You're capable of so much more.

It's time to step fully into your natural power and let go of everything that is holding your back. You're ready to do something that you've never done before: become who you are born to be.

The key is nature.

Fully and consciously connecting with nature is neither easy nor effortless. What stands in your way are the cultural and societal stories that you have unconsciously embedded within your psyche, along with the misconception that you've *already* experienced everything a connection to nature has to offer.

I'll let you into a little secret. You're not yet fully connected. You can go deeper. The true power of nature has yet to reveal itself to you.

I've spent the last five years figuring out how to teach this in a way that's accessible to everyone. At first I worked with people individually, tailoring the exercises and my approach to their specific needs. Then I developed a way to teach a group of people the same process in a far quicker and more powerful way, which allowed them to experience the benefits of consciously connecting with nature immediately.

This book comes from this work. It takes the concepts I teach and expands them so that you're able to start creating your own personal and planetary transformation by aligning your psyche with nature's wisdom.

Chapter One will get you to start thinking differently about nature. It delves into the essence and consciousness of nature, and considers the fundamental problem with Mother Earth. You'll learn how Aristotle's hierarchy of nature helped create a split between nature and humans in Western beliefs. Then we'll explore how quantum mechanics helps us see that the nature around us is a reflection of our inner nature, and how this can encourage us into a new way of sensing the world. I'll also reveal more about my own personal journey with nature.

In Chapter Two, you get an in-depth explanation of each part of The Nature Process along with how it works in action. This allows you to gain an overview of each part of the process and why it's important.

Chapter Three sees us diving into an explanation of natural presence. You'll discover how meditation and nature is connected along with how the earth connects to our brains. You'll learn about connecting to different aspects of nature and what Daniel Kish, a human echolocation expert, can teach us about our senses. You'll explore the reality of our sensory nature, discover how we have not five senses but fifty-four, and then start to experience them within both the city and the country.

In Chapter Four you'll build upon your knowledge of natural presence with learning all about your natural body. You'll learn how your body responds to stress and how your mind affects your body. You'll discover what horses have to teach us about body awareness and how our bodies naturally release energy. You'll then be guided to experience your own natural body before discovering how to connect to your natural body, along with the role emotions play in our body. Finally you'll understand how to connect your natural body to your natural presence.

Chapter Five leads you to discover the truth about natural attractions and why it's so important to follow them. You'll find out what cats have to teach us about natural attractions, and explore your working life and exercise in relation to them. Then you'll explore the insanity of civilisation and how this is manifested in all aspects of our lives right down to high heels and bras. You'll learn the truth about growth in relation to natural attractions and see how to discover the blocks within you. You'll then connect your natural attractions to nature before integrating this part of the process with the previous two.

In Chapter Six you'll start an exploration of natural communication, both as part of The Nature Process and by itself. You'll learn all about the Gaia hypothesis and how this facilitates communication between us and the earth, along with the story of Tilly Smith and how, through listening to her natural senses, she was able to save people's lives during the 2004 tsunami. You'll know exactly how nature communicates with us and be able to get permission to do so through a simple but effective exercise. You'll learn how to recognize the signs of consent from nature and explore the differences in natural communication with animals, plants, trees, stones, water, and even stars, before consolidating your natural communication fully into The Nature Process itself.

Chapter Seven will take you into the last part of The Nature Process and shows you how to experience a natural release. You'll discover how to use the energy of your heart to facilitate a powerful energetic shift within you that lets go of your emotional pain and limiting beliefs, and support this with the power of visualization. You'll read how I went through The Nature Process along with a reflection from one of The Nature Process Online's participants. You'll also learn how to fully integrate your experience into your psyche and receive some final reminders to help you as you get outside and do your own Nature Process!

In Chapter Eight you're going to focus on the potential obstacles that may stop you from fully engaging with The Nature Process. Here you'll explore how you might distract yourself from doing it or how you may weaken its effect by not acknowledging how you truly feel. You'll consider how your own beliefs about nature might get in the way, along with how falling into the trap of "green" marketing can actually stop you from experiencing the full power of The Nature Process. You'll look at the language you use when talking about nature and how that'll influence how you interpret what your insights from nature, along with how to stop yourself from getting caught up in the negative aspects of nature. I'll encourage you to let your imagination run free and trust what comes along, and help you to stay in an open mindset that allows you to ask "what if?" as you consciously connect to nature. Lastly, you'll learn how to avoid accidently disconnecting yourself from nature while falling into the trap of still thinking that you're connected.

Chapter Nine will inspire and encourage you as it shows you how The Nature Process will help you to be the change you want to make in the world. You'll also discover what's possible as you continue to experience The Nature Process on an even deeper level.

This is a book that's designed not just to be read, but to be *experienced*.

It's going to be one "heaven" of a journey.
Are you ready?
Let's go!

Chapter 1: Think Differently About Nature

A human being is a part of the whole, called by us "Universe," a part limited in time and space. He experiences himself, his thoughts and feelings as something separated from the rest — a kind of optical delusion of his consciousness. This delusion is a kind of prison for us, restricting us to our personal desires and to affection for a few persons nearest to us. Our task must be to free ourselves from this prison by widening our circle of compassion to embrace all living creatures and the whole of nature in its beauty.
- Albert Einstein

When you think of nature, what comes to mind? Maybe you think of aspects of the natural world such as mountains, trees, animals, and rivers. Maybe you think of a beautiful landscape or a world that exists independent of humanity and our civilization. Maybe you even think of nature as wild and savage, or something that is far simpler than the complexities of modern life.

Nature is all this and more. Nature is the universe with all its incredible phenomena including stars, galaxies, black holes, and planets. It's also the magic at work that holds the universe together and the reality of our existence.

As humanity has evolved, we have forgotten the meaning of nature. We have reduced it to nothing more than a resource available to us to use as we see fit with no respect or regard for the consequences.

We are now waking up to just how badly we have treated nature. Growing concern about global warming and climate change has put humanity's focus back on nature and our relationship to it.

The problem is that we view nature from an anthropocentric viewpoint. In the past we studied nature as a way to achieve domination over it. Today we study global warming and climate change mainly in terms of the impact that it has on human activity. Whilst we talk about the changes we can make to prevent further damage to the earth, we study the natural environment mainly in terms of how it can benefit humanity. It's all about us.

By adopting an anthropocentric viewpoint, we've forgotten a fundamental truth of our existence.

We are part of nature.

To once again be in harmony with nature, we don't need to study it to find out how we can control it for our own benefit. We merely need to consciously reconnect ourselves to nature and align our thinking with nature's wisdom.

The Problem With Mother Earth

For thousands of years, the earth and nature have both been personified as a woman. The earliest evidence of this dates back to around 22,000 BCE in the form of the Venus of Willendorf. This small female statuette discovered in 1908 in Austria has voluptuous breasts and hips, and a protruding vulva. The statue has no feet and its head is covered by circular bands.

Nothing is known about where the statue comes from, why it was made, or what its significance is. While it's speculated that this figure and others like it represent fertility goddesses, we really have no idea what they mean and if in fact they were intended to represent nature as a woman.

But perhaps not coincidentally, throughout many different cultures and mythologies nature has long been personified as a life-giving and nurturing mother from which all life sprang.

For example, in Greek mythology Gaia was great mother of the earth and all the universe. In Roman mythology she was known as Terra. Sumerian mythology refers to Ki as the earth goddess, and in Egyptian mythology we had Mut, the primal mother of all who was born of none. The Māoris from New Zealand call the earth mother Papatuanuku, while in Inca mythology Mother Earth is known as Pachamama, whose literal translation would actually be "Mother Universe."

The earliest written literal references to nature as a mother are found in ancient Greek going back to the 12th century BCE. In the English language the first recorded use of term was in 1266, with evidence suggesting it was popular between the 5th and 15th centuries to personify nature.

As a way of understanding nature, medieval Christian thinkers narrowed their understanding of nature to mean something that had been created by God. They didn't class her as a goddess, merely a personification of the middle zone between heaven and hell.

This idea continued and was developed during the time of the Enlightenment in the 17th and 18th centuries. Reason and logic were the foundational beliefs of the Enlightenment. The previous ideas of the medieval thinkers linked nature to God, which made it impossible to examine. In order to study nature it had to become *separate* from God. What better way to do this than to feminize nature?

After all, it was a well-entrenched belief that women were soulless creatures separate from God. This logic forms the basis for our modern understanding of nature and has led to the environmental problems we face today as we exploit nature for our own benefit.

There is a call to return to the ancient feminine viewpoint of the earth as a sacred giver of life. The problem with this perspective is that its roots lie in anthropocentrism. All references to nature as a mother are ways in which humanity has defined nature in a way that we'd understand it.

Through the identification of nature as a mother, we exclude aspects of nature that don't fit with our understanding of what a mother is. Nature is so much more than a mother. It's more than feminine. It's more than human. The truth is that nature pushes the boundaries of what our mind can understand.

It is neither masculine nor feminine. It just *is*. It both gives life and destroys life, and it does both without conscience.

Nature engages in a complex, chaotic dance as it maintains itself in balance. This dance is beyond what we as humans with our minds are capable of understanding. Despite hundreds of years of scientific investigation, we are not even close to having the secrets of nature fully revealed to us.

It is only when we consciously connect to nature that we can begin to understand the beauty and magnificence of nature beyond Mother Earth as we experience the ultimate truth of it on a multi-sensory level.

We are not just *part* of nature. We *are* nature.

In connecting to nature, we connect to ourselves and discover the truth of what it means to be fully human. The power inherent within nature is our own.

The Consciousness of Nature

Within some philosophical, religious and spiritual approaches there is the belief that there is no separation between the spiritual and material world. They are one and the same.

These approaches also believe that it's not just humans who have a spirit. All manifestations of the natural environment—such as animals, trees, plants, rocks, mountains, rivers, thunder, and wind—have souls or spirits too.

Not only is this idea present in Buddhism, Hinduism, Paganism, Jainism, Shinto, and Serer religions, along with many traditional Native American religions, but Plato, the ancient Greek philosopher, developed this with the idea of the *anima mundi* or world soul.

In his written dialogue *Timaeus*, Plato put forth the argument that, "This world is indeed a living being endowed with a soul and intelligence... a single visible living entity containing all other living entities, which by their nature are all related." For over two thousand years, this notion has continued to flourish in the philosophy and religion of the Western world.

It has also caused great debate throughout the centuries that still continues to this day. Modern science has come to reject this notion, believing that the ability to be aware of either an external object or of something within oneself belongs solely within the realms of humanity.

It was Rene Descartes, the 17th century philosopher, who created the split between the spiritual and physical world that we still see reflected in current mainstream Western ideology. He did this by making the distinction that the mind along with consciousness and self-awareness was something different from the physical brain. Descartes argued that the mental components of the mind cannot exist in space and that physical objects are incapable of thought. His work served as validation for studying nature as something separate from God.

Yet evidence is increasing that contradicts both the idea of a split between mind and body, and that consciousness exists only in humans.

We are now discovering that animals such as dolphins, elephants, pigs, chimpanzees, gorillas, bonobos, and orangutans display awareness of themselves as being separate from their environment.

The standard measurement for this is through what's known as the mirror test devised by Gordon G. Gallup, a North American psychologist, whereby a part of the animal's skin is marked in a way that's only visible in a mirror. Awareness of self is assumed when the animal directs grooming behavior towards the mark.

Furthermore, animal cognition scientist Irene Pepperberg's work with captive African grey parrots has shown they possess near human-like levels of consciousness. They are able to use human language with meaning and perform abstract cognitive tasks related to shape, color, and number on a level equaling that of human toddlers.

There's even research emerging that shows that plants have a form of intelligence that allows them to sense, learn, remember, and react in ways which we humans would recognize.

In 2005, The Society for Plant Neurobiology was created after the first international symposium was held in Florence. The society points out on its homepage that plants exhibit behavior that is just as sophisticated as animals. Because this behavior occurs at a much slower rate than in animals, science has been unable to properly see it until now. Yet if we truly want to understand the world around us we need to learn to see plants as dynamic and highly sensitive organisms.

In 2014, there were a couple of amazing conferences that took place. In Ibiza, for the first time ever, there was a scientific conference on the research into Ayahuasca, a psychoactive plant medicine from the Amazon jungle. In London, a conference on plant consciousness took place that blended together the values of plant neurobiology, permaculture, deep-ecology, eco-psychology, shamanism, and herbalism.

Plant consciousness is no longer just in the realm of philosophical, religious, and spiritual traditions. It is now firmly placed in the sphere of science, and interest and research in the field continues to grow.

It also seems as if the mind-body split as identified by Descartes was wrong, and ancient philosophy, religion, and spirituality were right all along. There is already strong evidence from neuropsychology that shows that mental process such as attention, memory, reasoning, language, etc., have a physical basis in the brain. Research into the neurobiology of plants is finding that their intelligent behavior has a physical basis too. These discoveries are changing the way in which we view the world.

Aristotle's Hierarchy of Nature

Aristotle, another ancient Greek philosopher, was a student of Plato's who was devoted to natural science. His views shaped not only medieval scholarship but continued to impact the Western world until the time of the Enlightenment.

One of his biggest contributions was his classification of living beings, whereby he created a hierarchy, or *scala naturae*, that consisted of eleven levels, from zoophytes to man. Living organisms were classified based on the complexity of their structure and their body function. The higher up the scale you went, the greater the vitality and capacity for movement.

Like Plato, Aristotle also believed in the notion that all living beings had souls, though this was different to our modern day understanding of what a soul is. Aristotle's definition of a soul was similar to what we could call the life-force of something.

Aristotle believed that there was also a hierarchy of souls, with the living beings at the lower end of the hierarchy possessing fewer functions of the soul than those higher up the hierarchy.

It's here that our anthropocentric Western worldview begins. Aristotle placed humans at the top of the hierarchy, both in terms of their external capabilities and soul functions.

He stated that there were three types of soul: *nutritive*, which belonged to plants based on their ability to self-nourish and reproduce; *sensitive*, which belonged to animals who could both self-nourish and reproduce, and move and perceive their environment; and *rational*, which belonged to man and man alone. Man possessed all the soul qualities of plants and animals along with something uniquely his: intelligence.

It was this work that medieval scholars developed to create the Great Chain of Being. The Great Chain of Being was a hierarchal structure of all matter and life that was believed to be the way in which God had intended the world to work.

At the top of the chain sat God, and below him were his angels. The hierarchy descended through the stars and moons down into humans who were classified according to kings, princes, nobles and the common man. Below humans sat animals, themselves categorized depending on whether they were wild or domesticated. Then came trees and other plants, followed by precious stones and minerals before lastly coming to the earth itself.

The Great Chain of Being stated that although the earth existed, it was not alive, thus laying to rest Plato's notion of a world soul, along with any ancient religious and spiritual ideas of the earth as a living organism.

The Circle of Life was the ancient and universal tenet that the world existed in a cyclic nature with everything in life united, whole, and infinite.

With the acceptance of the Great Chain of Being, this ancient indigenous cultural view of the universe was broken.

Nevertheless, Aristotle still made a major contribution to our understanding of how the world works through the development of empiricism. This is a belief that knowledge comes primarily from sensory experience and is gathered through the processes of experimentation and experience. How we organize, identify, and interpret this sensory information is the way in which we perceive and understand the environment around us. As we looked at the world, this viewpoint provided a disciplined framework and helped expand our knowledge of how nature really works.

Nature Outside Reflects Nature Within

In the early twentieth century, the development of quantum mechanics by Albert Einstein and other scientists fundamentally changed the way we view the world. By bringing physical matter down to an atomic and subatomic level, we have been able to grasp the connection between energy and matter in a way we've never been able to understand it before.

Physical matter—the ordinary stuff we can see and touch—is made up of atoms. Atoms consist of particles known as protons, neutrons, and electrons. These particles are so small that atoms consist of mostly empty space. Despite the illusion of solidness with the human body, and everything else in the universe, it actually consists of more than 99.999% space. It's this space that connects us as humans to everything else in the universe. On a fundamental level we are all connected. We are all one.

Furthermore, the atoms within our bodies are continually exchanged with others in the universe. Physically, despite the illusion otherwise, your body is not the same body that it was a couple of years ago. The atoms within your body have been exchanged with those from stars, rivers, mountains, oceans, trees, and the earth itself.

Research also shows that once particles have been connected physically they stay connected even when they are separated by physical distance.

When a change affects one particle it affects any other particle that was one connected to it.

The implications of this have not been fully integrated into our current Western worldview. We still view ourselves as separate from the natural world around us, but this is a deeply flawed belief. The way that we try to control and dominate nature is the same way in which we try to control and dominate ourselves and others.

As quantum mechanics reveals the fundamental truth that on an atomic level we're all connected and are all one, we have to realize that if we're at war with nature, we're at war with ourselves.

And if we care for nature, we care for ourselves.

On an individual level, we fight a continuous battle between what feels good for us and what our society and culture have told us is good for us. We see this played out as we stay in jobs that don't fulfil us for the sake of money. Believing that they're not achievable, we sacrifice our dreams, and are encouraged to believe that owning more things will make us happy. We stay in relationships that aren't healthy and struggle with the demands of all the different roles we have in life. We hide aspects of ourselves thinking that they're unlovable and that we're unworthy. Yet all the time we're secretly dreaming of more.

This plays out on a societal level as we experience racism, sexism, and homophobia within our society, and conflict and war around the world. Instead of acknowledging the parts of us that we feel uncomfortable with, we project them onto others. We judge them as different from us and see them as the root of all our problems. If only *they* weren't different, we wouldn't have the problems that we do in life.

Global warming, climate change, deforestation, land degradation, intensive animal and crop farming, ocean acidification and pollution, and their negative health effects upon us, are the earth's way of warning us that we are fundamentally disconnected and out of balance, not just with the nature *around* us but also with the nature *within* us.

A New Way of Sensing the World

If we truly want to create planetary transformation and live in a world that benefits all living beings along with the earth itself, we have to start with our personal transformation and step into our own natural power.

That transformation starts with becoming aware that we are all one and acting from this place of unity. It's not just about understanding this on an intellectual level; it's about embodying this on a cellular level.

Unfortunately most of us are disconnected from our own bodies because we've been taught to hate them. In particular, we see this reflected in the unhealthy and unrealistic attitudes towards women's bodies in the media. Women, and increasingly men, are taught to judge their bodies by some unrealistic image of perfection that we're never going to live up to but are told that it's important to achieve.

Furthermore, we've been taught that our bodies and their natural functions are dirty. Things like burping and farting are considered impolite and disgusting. Crying is seen as being too emotional and a sign of weakness. Never mind the conditioning that we've received that has told us that it's wrong to feel pleasure in our bodies!

Instead we've been trained to be overly dependent on our minds, which run riot with all the voices of the social and cultural conditioning that we've received ever since we were born.

When we stay in our minds, we don't have to feel the pain from all the unhealthy conditioning we receive. In some ways it's easier. Going into our bodies and feeling the pain of our mental anguish on a physical level can be intense, especially when we try to face it ourselves.

That's where nature comes in. Nature's way of communicating is non-verbal. It communicates on a full sensory level, and the only way in which we can truly understand what nature is saying is by experiencing this communication through our bodies.

When we allow this communication in, we become fully supported by nature as we easily and effortlessly let go of any emotional pain or limiting beliefs that stop us from experiencing the truth of who we are.

We are able to give our pain to the earth and allow it to be recycled into something new. Yet many of us are afraid to do this. We view the earth as weak and fragile and as something that needs to be protected. The truth is dramatically different.

The earth is far more powerful than we give it credit for. Think of the power of a tornado or of a volcano erupting. The earth can create new landmass in a matter of days and destroy existing landmasses in a matter of minutes.

In contrast, our emotional pain and limiting beliefs are nothing more than a tickle of discomfort for the earth before the energy that we release into it is transformed anew into something that supports not only the earth's growth but our own.

The earth welcomes our pain because it's through our pain that the earth experiences itself. It has the capability to take our pain and transform it into ecstasy, which is then given back to us when we view a brilliant ball of red fire as it rises across the earth's horizon or when we splash in fresh, cool water, feeling its wetness against our skin. In this way we re-create the Circle of Life and allow ourselves to truly experience the nature within us and without in a way that sustains life rather than destroys it.

The earth has been in existence for 4.5 billion years, and nature—the universe—has existed for 13.7 billion years. In contrast, we humans, in our modern form, have walked this planet for a scant two hundred thousand years. When we allow ourselves to experience a full-bodied connection to nature, we allow the ancient wisdom that is inherent within it into our lives, so that we create not only personal transformation but planetary transformation as we re-birth the world.

Now this might seem too simple to you, and your mind with all its conditioning might want to discount what you've just read. Be aware of that and suspend your disbelief. Experience The Nature Process for yourself first.

I'm aware that I've presented an oversimplified view of human life in this chapter. I could have written an entire book based on the themes I've discussed in this chapter. The idea is not to dive deep into these issues with all their complexity, but to give you enough information to consider that there might be a different way of thinking about nature.

Your mind might to want to argue with what I've written, to find holes that will disprove what I've said here so that it can reinforce its belief in itself as superior. After all, that's what you've been trained to do your whole life! Don't fall into that trap. Stay open to the material that's presented in this book and engage with the process.

When you do, you'll discover a whole new way of being within yourself and within the world. You'll be open to the magic and mystery of life, fully nourished and supported by nature itself as you live out your greatest dreams.

My Journey Back to Nature

I've always been a bit of a nature geek. It comes from spending most of my childhood growing up in small villages. If I wasn't inside reading a book, you'd find me outside. It was an era when you'd take your bike and see how far you could cycle. Your only commitment was to be home for tea. It was a time of adventure and excitement, and it saddens me that this isn't a typical upbringing for everyone, especially nowadays.

We always had pets growing up. The cats' favorite place to sleep was on my bed. The doctor told me that it wasn't a good idea, as it would make my asthma worse. Because the cats said it was ok, I ignored him. Turns out that they were right. Research now shows that being exposed to nature helps boost your immune system, and that the best activity for a child who experiences asthma and eczema is getting down and dirty in nature.

As I grew up, I spent more time with cats than other children. My entire life has been one of not fitting in with people but being perfectly at home with nature. I preferred to be out in nature myself. It was the only time I felt comfortable and truly at peace.

The world didn't make sense to me. I couldn't understand why people were starving and the environment was being destroyed, yet nobody seemed bothered by it. Every year I took part in World Vision's twenty-four-hour famine fundraiser, because even as a child I couldn't watch what was happening in the world and do nothing.

My teenage years were painful. I so desperately wanted to fit in. I stopped talking about nature to others when my best friend at the time asked me how many friends I actually had. When I told her that the cats were my best friends, she scornfully replied that they weren't real friends.

At the same time I was researching into environmental activist groups such as the Animal Liberation Front and the Sea Shepherd Conservation Society. While their direct action approach was appealing, there was something about the use of violence in defense of the earth that didn't resonate with me.

Whilst walking out in the woods I received the insight from nature that if I truly wanted to change the system, I had to be part of it. This left me feeling confused and unsure about how I could make a difference in the world.

So when I discovered drugs and alcohol, they initially seemed a way of fitting in. Instead they became a way of numbing myself to the pain I felt inside. They also numbed my connection to nature, and I gradually forgot about it.

I left home when I was seventeen. My behavior was challenging for my mum and I blamed where we lived for all my problems. I thought that moving to the city would mean that I would escape my problems too.

That's not exactly what happened. I still experienced similar problems, but with drugs and alcohol I was able to numb my way through life and keep surviving.

That's where I was when my brother Peter died. High on drugs and just floating along, struggling to keep my head above water.

After Peter's death I returned home to stay with my family for the summer. It wasn't just a return home. It was a return to nature.

I rediscovered everything I'd forgotten about as I'd escaped the pain of my past by moving away. In blaming the place I grew up in as the source of my suffering, I'd disconnected myself from the strength and solace I'd received from the land around me.

Just like before I'd left I went to the woods to deal with the pain I was experiencing, and spent hours walking around. Then I'd spend hours just sitting outside staring at the stars in the sky. As I did, something within me re-awakened.

I started to sense that the trees were communicating with me. I had no idea what they were saying. Jumbled images, sensations, and thoughts crowded my mind. Yet even in my confusion I felt peace and comfort.

Combined with the experience of sensing my brother's spirit still around me, I felt as if I were losing my mind. I couldn't explain what was happening to me and other people around me didn't understand.

The next few months were an internal battle. Grief and peace raged within me and I had no idea how to reconcile the two. To kick-start that process I shaved my long red hair off to become completely bald before spending three days in a psychiatric hospital.

At the same time my mum and I realized that I always became depressed during the dark months of winter. We invested in a light box to see if that made a difference. It did.

This reaffirmed that I had a connection to nature that I didn't fully understand. The only thing that was certain for me was that if I felt peace in nature, then I had to spend more time there.

In the city of Edinburgh, where I lived, I started looking for nature. Thankfully it wasn't hard to find. There were pockets of woodland hidden throughout the city, with a canal that ran through it.

By the time I returned to university after taking two years out after my brother's death, I was spending regular time in the nearby wooded areas close to my home and at university.

I eventually gave up taking the bus to my work at the psychiatric hospital, instead preferring to spend an hour on foot (or thirty minutes on the bike) traveling along the canal to arrive there. This gave me two hours a day to be outside in nature.

Even in winter. *Especially* in winter.

There are so many stories about staying away from deserted places in the city. Perhaps ironically, I was safer walking along the desolate canal than I would have been in the city streets themselves. No one else was ever there. I had the place to myself.

Despite spending hours of my day outside in nature, I still felt something was missing in my life. By the time I finished university I felt trapped.

Trapped by the charity I'd created.

Trapped by the limitations of staying in one area.

Trapped by the potential future of actually going ahead to do a PhD in clinical psychology and working within a mental health system that, for me, didn't always support the needs of the patients.

I was working crazy hours. I gave all my time to the charity for free. It was an act of love for my brother, or so I told myself. I worked full time at the local psychiatric hospital and ended up doing nightshift for a while. I was tired and burnt out.

Something had to change.

One day I saw an advert on the internet for a holiday in Spain. All I had to do was pay for my flights and speak English to Spanish students, and in return I'd get five days in a five-star hotel for free.

I nearly didn't go. I mean, a foreign country by myself where they don't speak the language? Was I off my head?

Yet the more I thought about it, I realized that it would be a challenge.

Something new.

Something exciting.

Something that I'd never done before.

The fact that my brother's nickname was Pedro, which is Spanish for Peter, convinced me to go.

Those five days changed my life.

I stayed in a small rural village with a wide river running through it. Everywhere was green and alive. The hotel garden was filled with butterflies, darting from flower to flower. The warmth of the sun was unbelievable. The land spoke to me in an even deeper way than the land had in Scotland.

Before I knew it I had applied for a job teaching English. Nine months later I moved to Spain to start a new life.

After two months teaching English I was promoted to co-coordinator, though I still had to teach. I ended up in a beautiful part of Spain called Galicia. Known as the land of a thousand rivers, it's shrouded in mist and magic. It also has Celtic roots, so I felt very much at home.

Teaching English full time was demanding and left little time for me. I worked from nine in the morning until six in the evening. All this time I was teaching. The method the company used was intensive, focused, and demanding. Any additional paperwork had to be done in our own time. The time I spent in nature gradually decreased until I was lucky if I had two hours outside a week.

After two years I found myself in the same condition I'd been in before: tired, stressed, and burnt out. I took a month off work and spent as much of it as possible out in nature. Immediately I began to feel better. Yet it was more than that. I could sense that there was something even more powerful and magical about nature than I'd ever experienced before. This is when I had my experience with the old oak tree that I mentioned in the introduction.

Over the next few months I saved and planned as I created my exit strategy from teaching English. I got myself a coach, started coach training myself, and found another job in a nearby town with fewer hours so that I could devote more time to doing what really inspired me.

I also started spending more time out in nature again until I was back up to more than two hours daily outside. The insights I received led me to start my Masters in Applied Ecopsychology so that I could figure out how to share what nature was teaching me.

The grief I'd felt over the death of my brother might have been transformed, but there were other challenges ahead. My eczema flared up until it covered eight-five percent of my body. My relationship with my Spanish partner was breaking down. I loved Spain but I knew I needed to return home to Scotland.

The next year and a half was a period of deep healing for me as I built my business up around grief and healed my relationship with the land in Scotland. This was a time of rebalancing my mind, body, and spirit with nature's support. As this happened I realized that I was no longer attracted to working in the field of grief despite just having published my first book about it and spending the last couple of years rebuilding my credibility in the field.

I stopped taking on new clients and got another job teaching English, this time in Barcelona. It was a testament to how far I'd come. Not only did I manage to teach English full time but I also managed to maintain my connection to nature despite living in one of the most densely populated cities in Europe.

My situation gave me the time and space to allow my business to evolve into the work I do now. When I knew my time in Barcelona was coming to an end I started thinking about where I needed to go next.

Through a series of synchronistic events I was led to the island of Ibiza. Having made the decision to move there before I'd even been there, I thought I'd better go and visit.

I only had one day. I quickly found my accommodations before spending nine hours driving around the island visiting many different natural spots. The energy of the nature there was so high that by the time I'd left I'd spent most of my visit in an altered state of consciousness.

The six months I spent there—from January to July, 2014—were the most incredible of my life. What I learned from nature there became rocket fuel for my life and business. In the introduction, you read the results I got. Throughout this book you'll also find insights and examples from my own experiences with The Nature Process.

Whenever I feel blocked I go to nature. The process you're about to learn in this book is the same process that I use daily in my life. In fact as I type this I'm sitting at the top of a mountain in Andorra, the landlocked microstate in southwestern Europe, located in the eastern Pyrenees mountains and bordered by Spain and France.

I think about it now: The sky is bright blue with soft, fluffy clouds. While it's warm there's a gentle breeze that causes the long grass surrounding me to dance in joy. Everywhere I look there are mountains, many of them covered in trees. A cricket chirps and a bird calls.

It brings chills to the very core of my being. My shoulders ache slightly from the sunburn I got yesterday and my legs feel the rough pressure of the stone I'm sitting on.

Just before I started writing this, I was attracted to a rock that I saw in the distance on the mountain. I could feel its presence calling me. As I walked towards the rock I received permission to climb it. The rock had to be at least six feet in height.

I found myself drawn towards one of its corners. There in the rock face was a small ledge. As I attempted to climb it for the first time I felt fear rise up within me, and my foot slipped off the ledge.

Undaunted I tried again. As I felt for a handhold in the rock part of it came away in my hand. Scary. Yet underneath the fear was trust. I used all my senses to find the right way to climb up the rock and the next thing I was standing on top of it.

As I looked around, the rock communicated with me that I was to jump off it and land on a certain point in the soft grass. I immediately thought, eh no. That looks far too high. I felt a sense of powerlessness and hopeless rise up in me. Here I was stuck on top of a rock like an idiot with no way down.

I sat down on the rock and started speaking angrily to it. Thankfully no one was around to witness what undoubtedly would have looked like a crazy girl arguing with a rock!

As I ranted and raved at the rock I realized that my journey up the rock was a metaphor for how I was feeling about the launch of the Tree of Transformation program I mentioned in the introduction.

With this insight my fear dissipated. I already knew how to get down. The rock had told me. Excitement rose up within me as I went to the edge of the rock and jumped. I landed safely on the grass just as the rock had said.

Clearly I heard the rock say, "Again!" This time I had no hesitation. I quickly climbed up onto the rock again and this time enjoyed standing for a moment on it. As I looked down to where I was to jump off I still felt some discomfort rise within me. Yet I jumped again and landed safely.

Emboldened, I needed no encouragement to do it again. I climbed immediately up the rock, moved straight over to the edge, and jumped without hesitation. This was one of the most powerful lessons I had ever received from nature, and when you think about it all I really did was climb a rock and jump off.

That I can communicate this to you from here through the words you are reading right now is magic. Everything you've ever wanted is right there waiting for you through a conscious connection to nature.

I invite you into my world so that you too can discover how to consciously connect with nature and step into your natural power.

Your journey starts on the next page.

Chapter 2: The Nature Process

A new type of thinking is essential if mankind is to survive and move toward higher levels.

- Albert Einstein

The process I'm going to reveal in this chapter really isn't my own. It belongs to nature. It's what happens naturally when we are open enough to consciously connect with nature and be guided by it.

The problem is that most people today aren't able to experience this naturally. Through no fault of our own, we've become too disconnected from nature. Modern civilisation has created a fundamental disconnect from nature within our psyche that isn't even acknowledged as the root of all our personal, social, and environmental crises.

Now that's a pretty bold statement to make. I am aware of that.

Remember, nature has existed for 13.7 billion years. The Earth has existed for 4.5 billion years. In that time both nature and the Earth have managed to keep themselves in balance. This is a 100% success rate in growth and transformation. We can learn from that.

It's only by realigning ourselves with nature's wisdom that we'll be able to not just survive individually and collectively, but to truly thrive as people and as a planet.

Outlined below is the five-step process that helps you shift your emotional pain and limiting beliefs with nature's support so that you can step into your natural power.

1. Natural Presence

The Nature Process starts with your tapping into your natural presence. This is the ability to exist fully in the moment with a deep awareness of the nature around you. It's the ability to silence the chatter in your mind and observe on a deep level the relationships that exists between different parts of nature.

It's part of what some people might call mindfulness, which despite its spiritual association is nothing more than an awareness of what's happening in each and every moment of your life. It is a mental state that allows you to acknowledge and accept, without judgment, feelings, thoughts, and sensations as they arise.

However, natural presence goes beyond mindfulness. The main focus of natural presence is the natural world that exists around you. It's the ability to experience nature without your sense of self blocking that connection in any way, shape or form.

Through natural presence you develop the ability to experience each and every moment without attaching a story to it as a way of explaining what is happening. This allows you to break free from the past, forget about the future, and focus on the only place your natural power exists; the present.

Your success with The Nature Process depends on your ability to master natural presence as fully as possible. The deeper your natural presence, the more powerful the results you'll receive as you let go of your emotional pain and limiting beliefs.

While natural presence is part of The Nature Process, it is also something that independently exists within its own right. That's how powerful it is.

Imagine that you are an alien recently landed on earth in the middle of the wilderness. Nothing is familiar. You don't know the labels that humanity has given to the natural world that you're witnessing. You don't know how anything works. What would you do?

You'd explore the natural world through the senses you have. Your natural curiousity would allow you to experience the world as it is, without preconceptions.

In order for you to develop your natural presence you need to experience your awareness of the earth as if it were the first time you'd ever encountered anything like it.

2. Natural Body

Once you have connected to your natural presence, you turn your focus to your natural body. This is the ability to be fully present in your body and experience it without inference from stories or judgement. It's the ability to take natural presence and turn it inwards on an embodied level so that you can experience the nature within you to the same extent you experience the nature around you.

Our bodies have their own innate wisdom. They know exactly what they need to do to remain balanced and healthy. Yet most of us are disconnected to some extent from this wisdom, which leads to injury and disease.

Right now, as you're reading this, there are a multitude of processes that you are not aware of occurring within your body to keep it functioning.

A lot of these processes involve other organisms. Ninety percent of your cells are made up from microbes and not human cells. Your body is actually a mini-earth capable of sustaining life for more than 90 trillion inhabitants.

It also acts as a natural antenna that allow us to pick up the electromagnetic frequency of the earth and allow our minds to make sense of the non-verbal communication that exists between us and the planet.

Your natural body is the key to making The Nature Process work for you. It's through your body that you will let go of your emotional pain and limiting beliefs, and give them to nature to be recycled into something new that supports both you and the planet.

First, though, you have to understand how your body works and then re-learn to listen to your body's wisdom.

3. Natural Attractions

Connected both to your natural presence and your natural body you then start to focus on your natural attractions. These are the building blocks for the existence of nature and life as we experience it. These are what initially caused the universe to blink into existence, expand, and grow. They are what caused the Earth to form and life to develop on it.

Quantum physics shows us that on a molecular level everything that we see and touch is nothing more than atoms and particles vibrating at high speeds in such a way that they create physical objects.

Natural attractions are the space that exists between these atoms and particles and the pull that brings them together to create solid objects. 99.99% of everything, including ourselves, is made up of natural attractions.

In this way, life exists in an interconnected web with everything in existence related to everything else. In order for us to fully experience life all we need to do in each and every moment is follow the pull of these natural attractions. This is how nature has a 100% success rate in growth and transformation.

As part of The Nature Process, natural attractions guide us to connect with a part of nature that can give us the support we need to let go of our emotional pain and limiting beliefs easily and effortlessly. This is how we ensure that each and every time we consciously connect to nature we are brought back to a state of balance and harmony.

When we become fully present to the nature around us and the nature within us through natural presence and natural body we also become fully present to natural attractions and are able to harness their power and make it our own.

You do this by establishing a connection between the thoughts, feelings, and sensations you experience in the moment and whatever part of nature you are drawn to in that same moment.

That part of nature has a message about the truth of who you are, and reflects back to you the highest part of yourself that your fear and doubts tend to hide. By ensuring that you focus on a part of nature that makes you feel good, you guarantee that you're also accessing the highest part of yourself too.

4. Natural Communication

Once you resonate with a part of nature through your natural attractions you then move into a state of natural communication. This is the ability to experience and understand the way in which nature communicates with us.

We listen to nature through our natural presence and our natural body. This allows us to experience and understand the non-verbal sensory way in which nature speaks to us.

Our ability to experience the natural communication of nature is present from the moment we are born. Yet our society and culture weaken this ability as we grow up. As adults we need to re-learn this unconscious ability and make it conscious. We do this by learning how to translate the communication that we receive from nature through all of our senses.

Humanity, in general, currently interacts with nature from a place of domination and oppression. We view the earth and its non-human inhabitants as natural resources available for our use whenever we want.

Our natural communication enables us to shift from this perspective into one of consent and co-operation with nature, which in turn amplifies its healing and transformative abilities.

As part of The Nature Process, natural communication allows us to experience a conscious connection to nature that enables us to sense that we are part of the complex dance between all life on earth. It's through an awareness of this that we are able to let go of our emotional pain and limiting beliefs, and bring ourselves back into our natural power.

5. Natural Release

Once you have experienced natural communication with nature you are then able to move into a natural release. This is the ability to integrate yourself energetically with nature and allow the naturally high energy of nature to support you as you let go of your emotional pain and limiting beliefs.

Natural release works on a sensory level allowing you to bypass the neural pathways created in your mind from previous rumination of whatever thoughts are connected to your emotional pain and limiting beliefs. By not engaging with these thought processes it becomes easy and effortless to shift the body sensations associated with them.

Nature infuses you with its natural wisdom that guides you to a state of balance and wholeness. You don't need to do anything except allow this to happen.

For many, this is the most challenging part of the process. We've been taught throughout our lives that we need to *work* to achieve success. With The Nature Process, success comes from merely *allowing* nature to do what it does best.

Sometimes as I've guided people through The Nature Process I've heard them say during natural release, "But I don't know how to shift this." You don't need to know. Nature knows. All you have to do is relax and let it happen.

When used as part of The Nature Process, natural release offers you a safe and gentle way to let go of your emotional pain and limiting beliefs without getting caught up in them. You feel supported and nourished by nature as it guides you to discover the truth of your own natural power.

The Nature Process In Action

When all five parts of The Nature Process are put together, they become a seamless experience that you can complete within thirty minutes or less. The reason that I teach you to actively experience each part of the process separately and then build it upon the other parts is that your understanding of how it works will be far more complete.

The idea behind The Nature Process is that you successfully learn how to do this yourself without having to rely on other people to facilitate the process for you.

Now I'm not going to discount the power of personally being led through The Nature Process. When I've done this for people I've witnessed them go deeper into the process than they would have been able to do initially by themselves.

If you sign up to go through The Nature Process Online (www.thenatureprocessonline.com), you'll have the opportunity to have someone actually guide you through this process. Your guide will be a wise practitioner whom I've personally trained to ensure that they know exactly how to support you to get the most powerful experience possible.

You will be able to go deeper with The Nature Process if you have the support of an experienced facilitator.

You will be able to go deeper with The Nature Process if you join the online community and experience a different learning environment. The group support available will consolidate what you'll learn in this book.

It's not compulsory. We have been socially conditioned to believe that many things aren't possible without the support of other people. I didn't have anyone guiding and supporting me while I developed and initially taught this process, but I'm able to go really deep with it.

Nature supports me and it can support you too. The challenge you face with being able to accept nature's support is that you need to have a deeper relationship with it than you believe is currently possible. You have to be so comfortable with non-verbal communication that you can clearly understand it without effort. It requires a level of trust in nature far greater than you currently have right now.

As I've already shared with you, I've devoted twelve years of my life to consciously understand how to connect with nature. Before I started this on this path, I felt as if I had a connection to nature.

Twelve years later, I now realize that what I understand and can currently teach is just the tip of the iceberg in terms of what's possible through a conscious connection to nature.

To truly allow nature to fully support you, you have to explore and work through your own limiting beliefs around nature. To achieve that you first need to be able to use and understand The Nature Process.

It's really a bit of a paradox! Yet as you do this you will develop a relationship with nature that transcends any other relationship you have. One thing that is certain: To develop this depth of a relationship with nature takes time and repeated regular conscious contact.

The good news is that if you're reading this book then you're already further along the path than you realize. What you learn experientially as you engage with the material presented in the following chapters will accelerate your journey in the most delicious way.

Chapter 3: Natural Presence

The basic laws of the universe are simple, but because our senses are limited, we can't grasp them.

-Albert Einstein

This is the longest chapter of the book with a lot of information. And whilst what I'm sharing in this chapter could easily be a book in itself, I've kept the information simple so that it's easy to digest.

The reason there's so much information here is because I want to make sure that your mind has enough information to be comfortable and confident going through The Nature Process in full by the end of the book.

While natural presence might seem the simplest part of The Nature Process, it's actually the one that people struggle with the most. If you don't get a proper experiential understanding of your natural presence and realize just how deep you can become present to nature, then the rest of The Nature Process is not going to be as powerful as it could be.

This is the root of the process. The stronger and deeper your roots, the greater you'll be able to reach for the stars, step fully into your natural power, and be the change you want to make in the world

You'll know you've mastered natural presence when it becomes a part of your daily life and you don't need to make an effort to maintain it. You'll be permanently present and connected to nature 100% of the time. Whenever there's a disconnect, you'll notice immediately and move to reconnect.

The Connection Between Meditation and Nature

Meditation has become mainstream. It's no longer weird or woo-woo to talk about it. Researchers have begun to investigate its benefits, and are showing that meditation can help to reduce stress and anxiety. It helps us cope with pain and challenging emotions. It can boost our immune system and helps us get to know ourselves better.

All of this is wonderful, yet there's a mental block within many people when it comes to meditation. Despite there being many different ways to practice meditation, the traditional image that comes to mind is someone sitting cross-legged and trying to empty their mind to find inner peace. This stereotype stops many people from experiencing the benefits of meditation.

The drawback of meditation is that it invites people to go *within* as a way of receiving these benefits rather than simply focusing on what's already around us. What is incredible is that you can get the same benefits as meditation simply by going out into nature. In fact, you don't even have to go outside. Having a view of nature from your window can trigger some of the same effects.

One of my favorite groundbreaking studies was done by a researcher named Roger Ulrich in the nineteen-eighties. He was looking at patients who had been in hospital for the same operation. During the recovery after the operation, half of them were given a nature view. The other half saw only buildings. What was fascinating is that those who had the nature view experienced less pain, recovered quicker, and had fewer complications than those who just had the building view.

Now, before you get excited and pull up an image of nature on your computer, this idea of a nature view was taken further and tested to actually see if technological views, as in computer images of nature, have the same effect. The research shows it is something about the actual natural view and the way that it is created that supports us. You can't just look at nature online, like so many people do with TV documentaries. You have to be looking at the real thing to get these benefits.

When we do go outside, the benefits increase even more. Nature starts interacting with us on a physical level. Plants and trees produce chemical compounds called phytoncides, and when we're outside and surrounded by plants we breathe them in. These chemicals help boost our immune system and help reduce stress. There's even bacteria in soil that triggers the production of serotonin in the brain!

The Earth's Connection to Our Brain

It's not just on a physical level that nature is able to connect with us. It's on a mental level too. Within the earth's electromagnetic field there are a set of electrical discharges known as the Schumann resonances that occur naturally between the earth and the ionosphere.

These frequencies were originally discovered by Nikola Tesla, the man who invented much of the twentieth century technology that we have now come to rely on. Ahead of his time, this discovery was ignored until the 1950s when a physicist named Winfried Otto Schumann scientifically measured and confirmed that these discharges existed at a frequency of 7.83Hz.

Within our brains we have electrical discharges too. In fact, this is what enables our brains to transmit information through our neural pathways. The type of information we receive is varied by our brainwave frequency.

Research shows that we have four different brainwave states measured by their frequencies; the Beta, Alpha, Theta, and Delta states. I'm only going to talk about the first three states here.

The state that we spend most of our time in is the Beta brainwave state, which functions at a rate of 14-40Hz. This is the fastest brainwave state when we are most alert and our minds are most active. This is the state that we're in when we experience stress and anxiety, when we're working on trying to reach a deadline or dealing with the challenges of modern life. It's the state we're in when our inner voice is the loudest.

Then we move down into the Alpha brainwave state, which functions at a rate of 8-14Hz. This is where we start to experience relaxation. Our mind becomes quieter and we enter a meditative state. Yet we're still alert and focused. A lot of research has focused on the benefits of entering the Alpha brainwave state as we're able to receive inspiration along with enhanced learning.

When our brains enter the Theta state this is where magic happens. This brainwave state functions between 4-8Hz. In this state our mind becomes still and we experience silence. Total silence. Our conscious mind is in effect switched off. This is the realm of deep knowing, intuition, visualization, of our connection to ourselves and to the world. This is where our natural presence lives.

It's no coincidence that the magnetic frequency of the earth is the same. Although controversial, this is why connecting to nature is so powerful. When we go outside and become conscious of nature we're able to connect with the frequency of the earth and bring our brains into sync with that energy. It becomes easy and effortless for us to drop into the Theta brainwave state.

This is where we need to arrive first in order to experience a powerful letting go of emotional pain and limiting beliefs with The Nature Process. Research into the different brainwave states shows that when we're trying to change our behavior or create new thought patterns, it takes thousands and thousands of repetitions in the Beta brainwave state.

If we change our behavior or create new thought patterns while in the Theta brainwave state, we only need one or two repetitions to create successful change. We can let go of all the obstructions that are stopping us from stepping up into our natural power easily and effortlessly when we use a connection to nature. A connection to nature supports us with our growth and transformation and helps us to tap into the essence of who we truly are.

Incidentally, children up until the approximate age of seven spend most of their time in the Theta brainwave state. This is why unconscious childhood crap is so difficult to leave behind. We're trying to remove deeply ingrained behavior learned while in the Theta brainwave state through working on it while in a Beta brainwave state as adults. Duh! No wonder change seems difficult at times.

Connecting to Different Aspects of Nature

So far I've just been talking about developing your natural presence within nature in general. Yet within nature itself there are many different parts that make up the whole.

Not only are there living plants and trees to connect to, but there are also seemingly inert things like rocks and rivers. Each of these has a different frequency that affects our ability to connect with them.

Plants and trees have a higher frequency than rocks and rivers. It is easier for most people to connect with plants and trees rather than rocks and rivers because of the differing frequencies of these parts of nature.

Rocks and rivers are closer to the last brainwave state, which is Delta. This functions at a rate of 0.5-4Hz and is where we experience a state of deep dreamless sleep and total relaxation.

It's already hard enough for most people to shift their brainwave states into the Theta state, especially if we've been in the Beta brainwave state for a long period of time. That's why I'd always recommend people to initially focus on connecting to nature through plants and trees. It's easier for us to do so.

Not only is the frequency of trees and plants higher, but they also have an ability to synchronize energetically with us. Whilst science is yet to fully explain how this works, one example of this is that when we actually go and put our hands on trees, the flow of their sap regulates to the same rhythm of our blood flow.

This is a beautiful example of the symbiotic relationship between ourselves and nature. It's one that helps us develop our connection to nature so that eventually we are able to connect to the deeper energy of the rocks and rivers.

The Difference Between Vibration and Frequency

You may have heard people talk about raising their *vibration*. Or maybe how nature itself has a naturally high vibration.

This is not the same thing as the *frequency* of your brainwaves, and the cause of potential confusion in fully understanding your natural presence.

Vibration tends to be a spiritual term that is connected to awakening and enlightenment, although it does have its roots in the natural sciences, namely physics.

Frequency refers to the number of times something repeats in a specific period of time. When we refer to the different brainwave states we are talking about the number of electrical charges released in that time period. The fewer number of electrical charges, the more you are able to connect with yourself and with nature.

Vibration refers to the amount of movement something has from its place of balance. When people talk about raising their vibration, what they mean is that they wish to reach a state of natural balance and wholeness. Nature is already balanced and whole. This is what is meant by nature being of a high vibration. If something is low vibration it means that it is in a state of imbalance and incompleteness.

The lower the frequency of your mind, the higher your vibration is in terms of your connection to the Universe, Source, God or whatever you choose to call it.

To put it another way, the deeper your connection to nature, the more you are in a state of complete alignment with yourself and everything that is. The way to experience this deeper connection to nature is through our senses.

Daniel Kish - Human Echolocation Expert

After having both eyes removed when he was thirteen months old after developing an aggressive form of cancer in his retinas, Daniel Kish has been totally blind. He's the president of World Access for the Blind, a non-profit organization whose mission is to help people with all forms of blindness create self-directed achievements and increase public awareness about what blind people are capable of doing. To date this organization has helped over 7,000 people in thirty different countries.

Despite being blind, Daniel still has the ability to "see." As a child Daniel taught himself how to use echolocation by clicking his tongue. This in itself is not remarkable. There have been other cases of blind people teaching themselves echolocation. What's unique about Daniel is that he's amazingly good at it, and he's the first person to have figured out how to teach this to others.

He teaches this technique to blind people through the work of his organization, and has also successfully taught it to people who are sighted. In 2009, a group of researchers from the University of Alcalá in Madrid conducted a study into whether it was possible to train sighted people to echolocate with Daniel's support. Despite some people believing the idea was ridiculous, the study showed that after just a few days of training, the participants had all gained basic echolocation skills.

Traditionally we've thought of echolocation in terms of how dolphins and bats communicate, but we've never thought of it as a human capability. Yet Daniel has been able to tap into his own sensory nature, connect this to the natural world around him, and develop a skill that is naturally ours by birthright.

Daniel models what he teaches to other people. He lives alone. He does not follow the norms that are commonly associated with people who are blind who are taught to keep their environment the same and adapt to that rather than let the environment adapt to them.

Daniel doesn't stick to familiar routines, nor does he use a white stick as his main method of "seeing." He's out there in the wild going camping by himself, climbing trees, and even mountain biking, and he's teaching others like him to do the same.

Just like any revolutionary approach that challenges mainstream thought, there's been a lot of criticism around what Daniel's doing. It requires time and commitment to achieve a high level of expertise in human echolocation. People don't experience immediate results, which leads those who are impatient to question the validity of this approach.

Why doesn't every blind person do this? In fact, blind children intuitively click their fingers, clap their hands and stamp their feet to make noise that will help them develop the skill of echolocation. But sadly, too often blind children are actively discouraged from doing this by their well-meaning parents, because this is not considered acceptable behavior in society. Think about it from your own perspective—how many times have you been told off for making noise that wasn't appropriate for where you were?

We are born as children knowing how to use our senses so that we can connect to the world. Unwittingly, not just in blind children but in all children we shut down these capabilities by training them to respond to social rules and behaviors that are not in their best interests.

I don't know about you, but I want to pull my hair out with frustration and scream loudly, "What are you doing?" But if I did, I'm sure I'd be ignored because it's not a socially acceptable way of communicating!

Daniel and his work remind us that we as humans have sensory capabilities far more powerful than we realize that allow us to connect to nature on a level that we have previously not thought possible.

The Reality of Our Sensory Nature

This is what the society that we live in has been doing to us. It's been shutting our senses down and stripping us of our ability to connect with the natural world around us. It's stopped us from connecting to nature and ultimately the very essence of who we truly are.

Within our culture and society it's been commonly accepted for thousands of years that we only have five senses. This belief is so persuasive that we accept it as fact and have never fully explored or challenged it.

Recently there's been the emergence of what some people call a sixth sense. This enables us to connect to a world that we can't see. It's the sense that leads people to say they can see ghosts, among other things, as popularized by the film of the same name with Bruce Willis.

Even this is wrong. We don't have six senses. We have in fact fifty-four senses.

Yes. You read that right. We've been taught to ignore forty-eight of our natural senses and discount any information we receive from them as valid.

This is why so many people have difficulty in connecting to nature. They've been unconsciously trained out of it by birth.

Now it's possible that you might be thinking something like, "Seriously? Are you sure? That can't be true? What?"

That's OK. Beliefs can be very difficult to change, especially when they're beliefs that have been accepted by a whole culture and society for thousands of years.

I can remember when I first discovered the information about the fifty-four senses through the work of one of my mentors, Dr. Mike. J. Cohen from Project NatureConnect. I read the information and didn't quite know what to think. So I put it down and didn't think about it. Yet something made me go back again and again to read the information before I finally realized I needed to go outside and explore this for myself.

It took me about a year from first discovering this before I actually signed up to study for my Masters in Applied Ecopsychology with Dr. Mike. His work seemed so radical and out-there that I was initially slightly wary of getting involved.

Dr. Mike has spent the last fifty years devoting his life to a sensory exploration of how a connection to nature affects our personal, social, and environmental well-being. His work is ground-breaking and challenges many scientific beliefs. It is ahead of its time and revolutionary, so much so that it's been excluded from mainstream science.

It's now time to dive into the fifty-four senses. When we become aware and conscious of these fifty-four senses in nature, more magic happens.

We start creating that shift into the Theta brainwave state that allows us to reach that state where we're completely connected to ourselves, to our intuition, and to Nature. We're able to create new life-changing habits and behaviors and let go of all that crap that is stopping us from being who we are born to be.

The Fifty-Four Senses

Our extended senses are those sensations, feelings, and thoughts that allow us to experience the world in a far deeper, more intimate manner than just the ordinary five. They are a non-verbal way for us to experience the world in which we live in. Our senses existed before we developed the capabilities of language. As Derrick Jensen, a North American writer and radical activist states, they are a language older than words. Our senses allow us to fully connect with the natural world around us and experience it through our mind, body, and soul.

There are four main types of senses: radiation, feeling, chemical, and mental. Each of these types offers us a different way of sensing the world. To aid your ability to understand and integrate the fifty-four senses into your own understanding, I've explained each sense here in more depth to help you explore the senses yourself.

This is where I want to offer you a challenge. Put down the book. Don't read ahead. Instead take a moment to discover how many senses you may unconsciously possess. Even better, go outside. If you take the time to explore this experientially you'll get so much more out of the rest of this chapter.

When I taught The Nature Process online I didn't give the participants the full list of the fifty-four senses until a few days after this module. I wanted to engage their curiosity and inspire them to get outside and explore their senses for themselves.

There's a risk that as you read this book you'll start to intellectualize the information in it. Your mind will read the information about the senses but you'll not actually take the time to experience them. It's only when you take new information and experience it fully that you truly understand what is being taught.

Also, if you start to explore the fifty-four senses without actually knowing what they are, you'll engage your mind more. Ask yourself the questions, "What are the fifty-four senses? How many can I identify?"

Research shows that our mind responds to questions. It engages our interest and makes us want to know the answer. Asking questions and actively engaging your mind makes it easier to synchronize your mind with your natural presence. This way your focus is already on nature making it easier for you to drop into the Theta brain wave state.

Radiation Senses

These senses relate to our ability to sense energy that is transmitted through waves and particles.

Sense of light and sight, including polarized light.

Look around you with your eyes. What you are seeing is a result of the sense of light hitting your retinas and creating visual images.

Sense of seeing without eyes such as heliotropism or the sun sense of plants.

This sense is strongest in those who like to sunbathe. It's the ability to orient yourself in line with the movement of the sun and see its location without even opening your eyes.

Sense of color.

Again look around. You'll notice different colors.

Sense of moods and identities attached to colors.

This sense comes into play when we decorate our homes. We choose different colors for different rooms depending on what emotions we want to evoke while we're in that room. This sense is one that interior designers draw on a lot.

Sense of awareness of one's own visibility or invisibility and consequent camouflaging.

In the army, this sense is used and developed to ensure that soldiers are better able to integrate within the environment that surrounds them.

Sensitivity to radiation other than visible light including radio waves, X rays, etc.

We might not be consciously aware of this sense but the effects of it can manifest as disease within the body. Exposure to X-rays causes radiation sickness and potentially cancer. This is why when there are radiation leaks like after the Fukushima Daiichi nuclear disaster, areas close to the site of the leak are evacuated.

Sense of temperature and temperature change.

You use this sense when you decide to put on or take off a jumper. It's also the sense that allows people to complain about how the weather is either too hot or too cold but very rarely perfect.

Sense of season including ability to insulate, hibernate and winter sleep.

This sense is more noticeable for those people who experience dramatic differences between winter and summer seasons. It's also the sense that can trigger Seasonal Affective Disorder in people. Modern society doesn't accommodate our natural tendency to slow down and hibernate more in winter. This creates a discord between what people are attracted to doing and what society expects them to do in winter.

Electromagnetic sense and polarity, which includes the ability to generate current (as in the nervous system and brain waves) or other energies.

The only time I've ever been aware of this sense within myself is when I had acupuncture. I could feel the tingle of electricity moving throughout my body between the needles.

Feeling Senses

These senses relate to our ability to sense physical movement.

Hearing, including resonance, vibrations, sonar and ultrasonic frequencies.

Take a moment and really listen to what's around you. You'll be surprised at what you tune out by turning down this sense. Very rarely are we ever in true silence. Think about your mobile phone. I keep mine on vibrate yet because I spend most of my time in "silence" I'm able to hear it vibrating when I'm upstairs and the phone is downstairs. Can you?

Awareness of pressure, particularly underground, underwater, and to wind and air.

If you're a swimmer or diver you'll be aware of how the pressure changes depending on the depth of water you're in. And anytime you're outside, you can sense the intensity of the wind and air through the pressure you feel from them.

Sensitivity to gravity.

This sense is obvious. If I didn't experience sensitivity to gravity right now I'd be floating in mid-air rather than firmly ensconced on a chair at a desk typing these words. The same goes for you as you read this book.

The sense of excretion for waste elimination and protection from enemies.

We all need to go to the toilet throughout the day. This is this sense coming into play. If you couldn't sense that you needed to go then you'd end up peeing yourself or worse.

Unlike a deer or other hunted animal, I haven't yet had an experience where I've needed to eliminate waste to protect myself from enemies. This is the only advantage of modern society that I can think of when it comes to our senses.

Feel, particularly touch on the skin.

You're probably sitting down reading this right now. Become aware of your feet on the ground and your bottom pressing against whatever you're sitting on. There. You've just tapped into this sense.

Sense of weight and balance.

As you read this book you are able to sense its weight. You're also able to balance the book in your hands so that you are able to read it with ease. Even as you sit upright reading you are using your sense of weight and balance to ensure that you don't fall over.

Space or proximity sense.

Pick any object where you are. Notice the space that exists between you and the selected object. That's you using this sense. We use this sense all the time we're moving to ensure that we don't bump into things.

Coriolus sense or awareness of effects of the rotation of the earth.

This sense relates to the fact that even though something may be moving in a straight line we perceive it as moving in a curve due to the rotation of the earth. For example, if you watch the moon for a period of time throughout the night it seems to move in a curve across the sky. Yet the moon stays relatively still and it's the earth that's rotating. It's also got something to with ocean currents and hurricanes but I'm not going to pretend that I fully understand that part of this sense or can even explain that part of it properly.

Sense of motion. Body movement sensations and sense of mobility.

Anytime you engage in any form of exercise this sense is activated. Even as you turn the pages of this book or hit the next page on your electronic reader you're using this sense. You also use this sense to notice the movement of other things.

Chemical Senses

These senses relate to our ability to sense what physical objects are made up of.

Smell with, and beyond, the nose.

This is our ability to sense the different chemical compounds of various physical objects along with the ability to discern whether they are pleasant or not. We have more capabilities of smell that we realize. Research has shown that blindfolded people have been able to follow specific smells across a busy universe campus.

Taste with, and beyond, the tongue.

It's not just about our ability with the taste of food it's also about the ability to taste the presence of certain chemicals in the air. Think about if there's a fire. You can breathe in and taste the smoke as you inhale.

Appetite or hunger for food, water and air.

There's so much information out there about what we should eat and drink and when we should eat and drink it. Yet so much of this information is actually disconnected from this sense. The only reason that we ended up being told that three meals a day was necessary is that this eating routine helped support the working times of the industrial revolution. Today this sense is so out of balance in most people. Emotional eating is a great example of this. People don't necessarily have an appetite for food but they still eat it, at great cost to their health. Even worse most of our air is so polluted that we've just adapted to breathing crap air which atrophies this sense even more.

Hunting, killing or food obtaining urges.

In the past we would hunt for food. Today we just head down to the local supermarket to satisfy this sense within us. Not only that, but we're so disconnected from our food sources now that the thought of hunting and killing their own food may disgust us.

Humidity sense including thirst, evaporation control, and the acumen to find water or evade a flood.

This is our ability to sense the amount of water vapor in the air. It's like going into a sauna and struggling to breath because the heat is dry. Then when you visit the steam room afterward, not only is the air different as you breathe it but your skin responds differently too.

Hormonal sense, as to pheromones and other chemical stimuli.

This is a sense that is weakened by our use of deodorants and our desire for cleanliness. Research has shown that men emit different types of pheromones that attract sexually compatible females. Despite marketing to the contrary, it's not the Lynx effect but the pheromone effect that gets men the girls.

Mental Senses

These senses relate specifically to our mind.

Pain, external and internal.

Mental or spiritual distress.

Sense of fear, dread of injury, death, or attack.

These three senses are grouped together because they represent an attraction to seek further sensory connections in order to support our well-being. They are signs that we are disconnecting from nature and from ourselves. Once we reconnect to nature, we reconnect to ourselves and these senses subside.

They are warning flags that clearly shout to us, "Hello! Something is wrong. You need to take action to change this!"

Yet what actually happens with these senses in our modern society? The majority of people tend to accept them as part of life and learn to become comfortable living with pain, distress and fear. We have so many cultural beliefs that stop us from doing something about it.

Think of the expression, "That's life!" It exists in English, Spanish ("Así es la vida"), French ("C'est la vie"), and no doubt in many other languages. This is a form of acceptance that whatever pain, distress and fear we experience is just a natural part of life that we can do nothing about. We've lost the ability to sense that it's a sign we need to reconnect to our other senses.

Procreative urges including sex awareness, courting, love, mating, paternity, and raising young.

This sense is pretty much well developed in all of us. Relationships and children consume most of our desires and goals in life. Just think about how much time teenagers think and talk about sex and relationship. Come to think of it, nothing much changes as we get older!

Sense of play, sport, humor, pleasure and laughter.

Sadly, this sense seems to weaken the older that we get. We're told that play is for children and many of us lose the ability to have fun and laugh the older we get. You know all about Grumpy Old Men (and women), right?

Sense of physical place, navigation senses including detailed awareness of land and seascapes, of the positions of the sun, moon and stars.

The more we've adapted to modern life with GPS technology, the weaker this sense has become. I can remember reading about people who ended up in the wrong place after their GPS let them down. They were so dependent on technology they couldn't even sense they were going in the wrong direction. I would laugh at this but I also remember the time that I got lost trying to find Princes Street in Edinburgh in my car even though I'd lived in the area for over five years at the time!

Sense of time and rhythm.

Tap your finger on your leg. Notice how you sense the rhythm. Tap faster and you'll notice this. You'll also find yourself noticing the time between each tap. Those who have this sense more highly developed include dancers and musicians.

Sense of electromagnetic fields.

This differs from the radiation sense in that it's a mental understand of how these fields work. Earlier I mentioned the work of Nikola Tesla. His sense of electromagnetic fields combined with the information he received from his radiation electromagnetic sense allowed him to develop wireless electricity and develop ways to allow electricity to safely pass through the human body. The only reason that this technology isn't in mainstream use is because Thomas Edison had more money and better marketing to discredit the work of Tesla. That's another book altogether.

Sense of weather changes.

Before we had weather forecasts, people were able to tell what the weather was going to do from observing minute changes in the weather. This sense is still active in many people who live in rural areas. For example, I can usually sense when it's going to rain. There's a combination of many different factors that include the appearance of the sky and changes in temperature and pressure that together indicate rain is not far off. I've not worked on developing this sense; it's just something that I naturally learned from being outside and observing nature.

Sense of emotional place, of community, belonging, support, trust and thankfulness.

As we've become more location independent through the rise of different modes of transport, this sense has weakened. Some environmentalists believe that the loss of this sense is directly responsible for the ecological crisis that we are now in. If you don't feel connected to where you are, you are less likely to want to take care of it.

Sense of self, including friendship, companionship, and power.

This sense means that you understand who you are along with who you consider to be the best people for you to associate with and how you express your ability to interact both with yourself and others. This sense is one that is severely challenged by modern society. Most people don't understand who they truly are and what they're capable of.

Domineering and territorial sense.

Probably one of the most developed senses in humanity as a whole. In a positive sense this can manifest as a parent's desire to do what is right for their child, even if the child isn't in agreement with the decision. In a negative sense this can and does manifest as war.

Colonizing sense including compassion and receptive awareness of one's fellow creatures, sometimes to the degree of being absorbed into a super-organism.

This is another sense that we've used collectively, though without the compassion and receptive awareness of our fellow creatures. The expansion of Europe into the Americas in the sixteenth century was fuelled by this sense. History shows us it was at the expense of our fellow creatures, both human and non-human, that colonizing occurred. Once we further develop this sense and bring it into balance we'll be able to create full awareness of how the earth and all its inhabitants are really one super-organism functioning as a whole.

Horticultural sense and the ability to cultivate crops, as is done by ants that grow fungus, by fungus who farm algae, or birds that leave food to attract their prey.

On a societal level this sense is represented by our agricultural industry and on a more personal level manifests through an interest in gardening, growing our own food, or even just having a nice bunch of flowers in a vase at home.

Language and articulation sense, used to express feelings and convey information in every medium from the bees' dance to human literature.

We've come to associate this sense mainly with spoken languages. I tell people that I've studied nine languages but can speak only three. This is a reflection of this bias within myself. I've also studied the language of music, numbers, dance, and movement, along with the language of cats, dogs, horses, and other animals that have captured my interest. Yet I don't include them in the number of languages I've studied.

Sense of humility, appreciation, ethics.

This sense allows us to decide what is right and wrong and gives us our ability to place ourselves in relationship to the world at large. If this sense is imbalanced, it gives rise to arrogance and narcissism or low self-worth and value.

Senses of form and design.

I would say that this sense is highly developed in architects, but considering some of the monstrosities that are passed off as modern design I'm not so sure. Historically this sense was evident in such constructions such as the pyramids or medieval castles.

Sense of reason, including memory and the capacity for logic and science.

This sense is directly responsible for the rise of philosophy, science, language and math over the last two to three thousand years. It's our ability to connect one idea to another. Sadly, not everyone is able to use this sense adequately and many a bad decision has been made from an overuse of this sense. The misuse of this sense alone has been responsible for the justification of oppression of women, gays, ethnic minorities, and all the other wonderful discrimination that exists in the world.

Sense of mind and consciousness.

Through this sense we are able to experience ourselves as individuals and experience the world as separate from ourselves. It's also the sense that when overactive gives rise to the phenomenon of what we call the monkey mind; that restless chaotic inner voice that constantly comments on what is happening both externally and internally.

Intuition or subconscious deduction.

This is the ability to acquire knowledge and information without logic or reason. It's that feeling in your gut that lets you know something is right without any evidence to back it up. It's the sense that most of us discount and find out it was right all along.

Aesthetic sense, including creativity and appreciation of beauty, music, literature, form, design, and drama.

In most of us this sense tends to be highly developed even though there is cultural conditioning towards what we sense is beautiful. For example, the ideal of feminine beauty has not only changed over time but depends on what part of the world you live in. Western society values thin as beautiful. Some parts of Africa value big as beautiful. I personally value everything as beautiful. After all, beauty is in the eye of the beholder!

Psychic capacity such as foreknowledge, clairvoyance, clairaudience, psycho kinesis, astral projection and possibly certain animal instincts and plant sensitivities.

Our wonderful sixth sense. Within this sense there are many differing levels of sensory capability. To be psychic is actually nothing more than having the ability to sense information not present to any of our other senses.

Sense of biological and astral time, awareness of past, present and future events.

Think back to one of your birthdays in childhood. Now think about how old you're going to be on your next birthday and what you'd like to do. This is you activating this sense.

The capacity to hypnotize other creatures.

Traditionally when we think of hypnosis we think of the stage magician getting people to run around like chickens and make fools of themselves. Hypnosis is actually nothing more that the ability to be able to put people into a state of hyper-suggestion. We all possess this ability, though it tends to be underdeveloped in most people. It can be used for good or for evil purposes; for example, this sense was highly developed within Adolph Hitler, and partially explains why he was able to convince an entire nation to commit horrible crimes.

Relaxation and sleep including dreaming, meditation, brain wave awareness.

This sense is pretty much self-explanatory, and is actually the sense we want to tap into to help us recognize when we are moving through different brainwave states. The more we can use this sense, the greater our ability is to end up moving into the Theta brainwave state with minimal effort.

Sense of pupation, including cocoon building and metamorphosis.

This sense is most commonly experienced by women during pregnancy. As they prepare for the birth of their child they find themselves creating a nest and gathering the necessary equipment and toys necessary for the metamorphosis into mothers.

Sense of excessive stress and capitulation

We all experience stress. It's probably one of the most developed and imbalanced senses in modern life. Too much stress shuts down our capability to function properly. We give up and tend to accept things because we no longer have the strength to overcome them.

Sense of survival by joining a more established organism.

An example of this sense manifesting itself in modern society is through people's desire to work for big companies, as they offer a sense of security and thus survival. In our ancient past this sense was connected to the earth. As feudal systems developed this sense was connected to aligning yourself with whoever had the most power and influence, something that still is at play today.

Spiritual sense, including conscience, capacity for sublime love, ecstasy, a sense of sin, profound sorrow and sacrifice.

This sense is where the development of religion comes from. When it's in balance, it guides people to develop compassion and love for other beings. When it's out of balance, it's responsible for the death and destruction of many other cultures, as we've been able to see throughout humanity's history.

Sense of unity, of natural attraction as the singular mother essence and source of all our other senses.

This goes beyond our sense of spirituality. It is the awareness of something that is impossible to explain in words and is frequently accessed by what Abraham Maslow, a well-known psychologist, called peak experiences. These are moments that stand out from everyday life. They tend to be profoundly impactful and can cause dramatic positive change in the way we view ourselves and the world.

Experience Your Fifty-Four Senses

You don't need to be outside to start exploring your fifty-four senses. You've probably started experiencing the senses even as you read through them all. If you were one of the people who took my advice earlier in the chapter, you put this book down and started exploring your senses beforehand.

If you are one of the people who just kept on reading (and don't worry because I'm one of those people too!) now is the time to start fully experiencing your fifty-four senses.

As individuals, our senses differ depending on the experiences we've had growing up. Some of us will have senses that are more developed than others. I probably have some senses that are stronger than yours and vice versa. Think of Daniel Kish; his sense of "seeing" without the eyes is incredibly strong. I doubt anyone reading this book could experience right now that sense the way he does.

We all have different ways of learning, too. These are connected to our senses.

If you're a visual learner, then explore the senses that relate to pictures and images.

If you're a aural learner, then identify the senses connected to sound.

If you're a verbal learner, look at the senses connected to words and language.

If you're a physical learner, explore and identify the senses connected to your body and a sense of touch.

The problem we face with our senses is that modern society has created an environment that deadens some of our senses and imbalances others. When we recognize this and start exploring our weaker senses, we are able to strengthen them.

Think about your sense of hunger and thirst. There's a lot of information out there about how people mistake their sense of thirst for hunger because they're unable to recognize the difference between the two. Maybe you're actually one of them. I know I used to be.

When you focus on exploring the difference between aspects of the same sense or different senses, you're able to discern the difference and enhance your sensory capability. Now I'm more than able to recognize the difference between thirst and hunger.

There is no right or wrong way to experience and explore your senses. There is only your way. We are all different. That means you need to explore what works for you.

Close your eyes. Explore what senses you can identify with your eyes shut. We take in a lot of information through our eyes. In evolutionary terms we've been trained to rely on our eyes, as they've been useful tools in helping us to sense potential danger. When we close our eyes, the senses that are more dominant are deactivated, so we have to start experiencing our other senses.

Once you've done this, open your eyes. Explore what senses you can identify like this and observe any difference.

Personally, I find it easier to keep my eyes open and to notice all the different senses I'm experiencing in that moment. I then focus on my ears and explore what senses I'm aware of through them. I very rarely close my eyes outside in nature, and when I do it's not for long. Other people who have participated in The Nature Process Online have commented that they have to close their eyes before they can open up their other senses. Play with this and find out what's right for you.

As you explore your different senses take a moment to label them. This helps keep the mind engaged so that it's easier to slip into the Theta brainwave state. Start an internal dialogue in which you consciously focus on saying, "Look at those leaves on the tree. I'm sensing the greenness of them and the round shape of them. I'm sensing movement as they're dancing in the wind. In contrast to the green leaves, the branches are brown, which again is my sense of color."

The more that you have this internal conversation with yourself (and it can be very powerful to actually verbalize it if no one else is around), the more you'll become aware of nature. The more you become aware of nature, the easier it is to drop into the Theta brainwave state.

It probably will be challenging for you at first, which is why it's so important to consciously engage your mind along with your sensory experiences. We're most used to spending time in the Beta brainwave state. Most people don't even believe that it's possible to experience silence of the mind. Even in meditation, teachers say that it's not about silencing the mind *per se* but allowing thoughts to arise without becoming attached to them. Play with your senses and discover the truth. Silence of the mind is possible.

If you have children, get them involved in this adventure. How much nature can you sense and how many senses are activated whilst you're doing so? Even the act of involving children is activating one of your fifty-four senses, if not more.

Don't underestimate the power of doing this on a regular basis. Developing your natural presence is not complicated, yet many people choose to make it so, especially by focusing only on one of their senses at the expense of others.

Make developing your natural presence part of your daily routine. When you leave your house, stop and take a moment to observe the nature around you. Every time you look out a window, stop and take a moment to observe the nature around you. Slowly but surely you will increase your natural presence.

When you have free time, make it a priority to get outside, even if it is just for five minutes. The more time you spend outside, the easier it will be for you to experience the Theta brainwave state whenever you sense nature. A short time is better than no time!

The Vibration of Our Natural Senses

Earlier on I mentioned the difference between frequency and vibration. When it comes to our natural senses, they too have different vibrations. Some senses have a higher vibration than others.

If you look at the last mental sense, which is a sense of unity with natural attractions and a recognition of all senses stemming from this one, you can see that this basically means a sense of how everything in nature is interconnected. Whether you call it Nature, God, or whatever you want, it is the highest vibration of all the natural senses.

This is a sense of being one with everything. Our brainwave frequency here is so low that our vibration is high enough for us to experience this. We're capable of experiencing everything that exists in the universe at the same time through this sense because it is the ultimate expression of all fifty-four senses functioning at the same time.

In contrast, think about another mental sense, the one of domineering and territory. The vibration of this sense is actually incredibly low, so we're able to access this sense when we're in the Beta brainwave state. We can see it coming unconsciously into play on a global level as nations and countries fight over natural resources and differing belief systems.

As we deepen our personal connection to nature, we are able to tap into other senses that have a higher vibration. This allows us to become multi-sensory beings who can use the balance and interplay of our other senses to turn down the effect of a sense such as this one.

Can you imagine what the world would look like if this sense were balanced with all the others? This is what we are aiming for with our connection to nature. Not just to fully experience life through the senses but also to experience all senses in balance with each other.

Explore Nature with Your Senses in Both the Country and the City

Traditionally, a lot of connecting to nature is focused on taking people out of modern day society over a period of a few days into the last remaining pockets of wilderness. The challenge with this is that not all of us have the time and resources to do this. It's also not necessary.

If we truly wish to maintain our natural presence, it's imperative that we're able to do this whether we are out in the countryside or within the city limits. We have to learn to live within the world as it exists now and develop a connection to nature no matter where we are in the world.

Some people have to commute hours to work. You need to be able to be present and aware of nature while you're travelling in your car. When you walk down a really busy and crowded city street, you need to be able to tap into and connect with the nature that already exists there.

Developing your natural presence in the countryside is really easy. Once you're there, there are no distractions. You simply throw your senses open and experience everything that nature has to offer. Dropping into the Theta brainwave state is relatively easy.

This is why most people who live there do not have a conscious awareness of their senses. They don't need to know about them. They can just experience them. It is also important to note that many people in the countryside are experiencing an eroding of their senses without even being aware of it. They believe that because they live in the countryside, they are fully connected to nature. As you'll learn in this book there's just a little bit more to it than that!

Developing your natural presence in the city is a whole different story. Not only is it far more challenging, but you also have to approach it differently. If you just throw open your senses and experience everything in the city, you become overwhelmed with negative sensory input that is damaging to your well-being.

In the year before I ran The Nature Process online, I was challenged by nature to live in Barcelona for a year. Barcelona happens to be one of the most densely populated cities in Europe and one of the six biggest.

As you know I'm not a city person. I grew up in a village of six hundred people. I've been a country girl my whole life. Even when I lived in Edinburgh, which is known as "the big village" because it's so small, I lived on the outskirts and hardly ever went into the center.

Living in the center of Barcelona gave me an opportunity to truly understand how you develop and maintain a connection to nature when everything around you is busy, bustling, and chaotic. If you live in the city, the chances are good that you don't have the opportunity to go for a two-hour walk through the forest every week. It's more likely that this is a special treat for you.

In order for you to develop your natural presence in the city, you need to experiment with the following techniques. These techniques also work for those who are living in the countryside as well and are a great way to deepen and expand your connection to nature.

First of all, you need to get house plants. You will learn a lot from having plants in the city. It's a wonderful way to bring nature into your living space. You can also bring them into your workplace. Research shows that productivity and creativity are boosted just by the presence of plants.

Secondly, you can't just throw open all your senses in the city. If you do, it's likely that all the noise and pollution will overwhelm your senses and actually make you ill. What you need to do is to focus on one particular aspect of nature. You pay attention to it and create a specific connection to this aspect of nature. This requires a little bit more focus than when you are out in the countryside due to the fact that there are so many other distractions.

In a city, one of the easiest aspects of nature to focus on is the sky. Observe this aspect of nature and explore what different senses you can engage to experience it. Challenge yourself to see how aware you can be of the sky throughout a certain time period. A reason why the sky is so powerful is that no matter where you are it's easy to sense the shifts from day to night. This shift triggers many different senses. If you look at the sky for long enough, and relax your eyes, you'll start to see a shimmering, translucent field over the sky. That's its energy field.

You can also focus on the wind in the city. That's nature too, and easy to sense whether you are inside a building or outside on the street.

In some cities there are a lot of birds. When you focus on them, what senses are you aware of?

Look at the sidewalk and see if you can sense any plants/weeds growing in the cracks and gaps.

Nature is everywhere. All you need to do is expand your senses to become aware of it.

Whether you live in the countryside or in the city, make this an adventure. Explore your fifty-four senses out in nature. This is how you incorporate your natural presence into your daily life. As you do this you will naturally reduce your stress levels and start experiencing life through a different lens.

Even if you go no further, mastering just this one part of The Nature Process will create fundamental changes in your well-being. That's how valuable this is.

Chapter 4: Natural Body

Body and soul are not two different things, but only two different ways of perceiving the same thing.

— Albert Einstein

You now have the foundation for The Nature Process through your deepening awareness of your natural presence. Having focused on the nature of the external world, it's now time to understand more about the nature that exists within you.

This chapter is designed to give you a basic understanding of how your natural body works. The more you engage experientially with the information in this chapter, the deeper your understanding of how your own body works will become.

We are all individuals, which means that there will be certain things your body does that are unique to you. I can't tell you what they are. You need to discover them for yourself.

While your natural body can be experienced by itself, independent of your natural presence, it's far more powerful to link the two of them together.

This is the catalyst of the process. The stronger and deeper your ability to experience your natural presence and your natural body together, the deeper your capacity for understanding your own natural power and what this means to you.

You'll know you've mastered the two parts of this process together when both nature and your body become such a part of your daily life that you don't need to make an effort to get outside and move your body in nature.

How the Body Responds to Stress

When we perceive an external threat to ourselves, we experience a hormonal response within our body. Adrenaline and cortisol are produced to help us cope with the threat at hand. These hormones cause physiological changes within the body.

Blood is pumped into our arms and legs, and our heart and lung capacities increase. We breathe more rapidly. Our ability to mentally process conscious thoughts is reduced. Digestion slows down or stops completely. We can experience shaking and flushing, and our hearing and vision are affected.

This is known commonly known as the "fight, flight, or freeze response." These changes occur to give us increased body strength and speed in anticipation what's to come. In today's modern world, this stress response is activated on a regular basis through traffic jams, stress at work and home, lack of time, money problems, and global crises.

Unlike in the past, once the threat has passed we are not effective in returning our hormone levels to their normal levels. In the 1970s, researchers at St. Vincent's Hospital, London, were the first to show that severe and continuous stress reduces the ability of our immune system to function effectively, thus making us more susceptible to illness.

Furthermore, if hormone levels remain high, they block our ability to produce serotonin, which is the happy drug that regulates our mood.

This leads not only to certain food cravings as the body attempts to rebalance the serotonin, but it can also cause stomach aches, shallow breathing, nausea, dizziness, sweaty palms, cold hands, lack of concentration, sleeplessness, anger and sense of being overwhelmed.

This stress response is the most important thing we need to understand when it comes to our natural body. When we understand how our body is functioning at a basic physiological level, we understand how to shift the energy within our body on a hormonal level.

If we do not balance our hormones, the imbalance creates disease.

How the Mind Affects the Body

Traditionally, a stress response was processed immediately within the body. The hormones were re-balanced and there was no lasting damage to the body's health.

Today we're experiencing something different that leads to stress being a huge problem for most of us. Not only do we have constant low-grade stressors within our lives, but we also tend to spend more time in the Beta brainwave state.

If you remember, this is when your brain is at its most active. The constant activity within the brain can interrupt our body's natural ability to process stress and life challenges.

The body is only able to exist in the present moment. It deals with stress and life challenges as they arise. Yet our mind has the capability of existing in the past, present and future. If your mind is firmly engaged in the past, it's unable to tell the difference between what is happening in the present moment and the past. Your body, and its hormone factories, can easily misread a situation and respond to a nonexistent threat.

When you think about challenges from your past, especially related to traumatic experiences, or worry about the future, the body responds as if it were real. This means that the stress response you initially *experienced* during an event is triggered every time you *think about* what happened.

How often do you get caught up in thoughts about what you could have done differently, or how some event in your past has affected your life? The brain in its Beta state can obsess over past events, taking you back over the event again and again and making you relive your experiences.

Your body relives them too.

This is what can block our natural presence. Even if we are out in nature, if our thoughts belong in the past or the future and they are causing us stress and anxiety, then our mind triggers a stress response that counteracts the effects of nature upon our immune system.

By staying in our minds, we block nature's ability to reduce stress and boost our immune system. This is why it's so important for you to engage your mind while you develop your sense of natural presence and why you need to first experience natural presence before you can truly experience your natural body.

If you are not fully present both to nature and to your body, you cannot truly experience your natural body and become fully conscious of its natural healing ability to shift emotional pain and limiting beliefs.

Horses: Masters of Body Awareness

In his book *Waking the Tiger*, Peter Levine posts an interesting question: "How on earth can a zebra can be out in the plains, get attacked by a lion, get mauled by a lion, yet the next day be out grazing and not affected by the traumatic experience?"

This question stuck with me because zebras are cousins of horses. They share similar processes in how they deal with danger.

Both zebras and horses are prey animals. This means they have to be fully aware of predators, because if they're not present to the environment and present to themselves by being in their body, they can end up getting eaten. It's a serious matter of life and death.

Horses are sensory animals with highly developed specific senses. It's what they rely on. Because horses are prey rather than predators, the way their senses have evolved to support to ensure they stay alive. They can hear noises miles away that we human are incapable of hearing. They can run fast, over long distances. They are also able to pick up information through the ground via their hooves.

When something happens that they perceive as a threat, which means their stress response is triggered, they instantly go into flight mode. This is their first natural response.

It's really interesting when you observe horses because they're able to read body language of people and other animals extremely well. That's what helps keeps them alive. That's why horses are being used in therapy. They have sensory capabilities beyond what humans are capable of, because humanity has developed by relying on its mental senses at the expense of other senses.

When I had my first experience with Equine Assisted Learning, I didn't know this. I spent a month at the Healing Hooves, Healing Humans, Horse Sanctuary in Sunnyside, Washington State a few years ago learning about Equine Assisted Learning as part of my Masters in Applied Ecopsychology. The founder, Betty Hames, was studying for her Masters in Applied Ecopsychology too. Together with another student, colleague, and friend, we integrated Equine Assisted Learning, Applied Ecopsychology, and coaching together to develop a powerful program that facilitates profound transformation.

I was really nervous because I didn't have a lot of experience with horses. As I went out into the corral to meet the horses they reacted to my fear. They started getting frantic, moving dramatically, running around and doing all this stuff that actually made my fear worse.

In contrast, a few days later I watched my friend who had grown up with horses go out and interact with them. One of the horses lay down on the ground, completely relaxed while the other horses welcomed him into their herd.

What fascinated me the most was watching what the horses did once they realized that the perceived threat had disappeared. I saw this happen again and again during the month that I spent at the horse sanctuary.

Whenever their stress/fear response was triggered, they wouldn't immediately return to a state of normal relaxation. There was a gradual process that they would go through. I watched as they would stop running and return to standing in one place.

Yet they weren't still. As they stood, their muscles would ripple and their bodies would shake. They'd stamp their feet, blow heavily through their nostrils, or breathe with deep sighs.

This really got me thinking about what Peter Levine said in his book about the zebras. It made me reflect deeply on how we process our own stress responses.

It also relates to what I said in the last chapter about blind children intuitively clapping their hands and making noise to try to teach themselves to see through echolocation, but parents and society stopping them from doing this.

The same thing happens to us with the ways in which we process our own stress responses. Just like the horses, we have our own physical ways that help us shift the energy of the stress hormones from our bodies. Yet we're prevented from fully rebalancing these hormones. We're told to sit up straight and don't fidget. It's not polite to burp in public, so we're trained not to do that. Our behavior patterns have been separated from our natural body by what we consider appropriate social behavior. Unlike horses, many of us are not able to rebalance the hormones of the stress response within our body. Instead we keep them elevated, weaken our immune system and ending up in a state of disease, which is an extreme imbalance within our body.

How the Body Naturally Releases Energy

There are many different ways in which our bodies are capable of releasing the hormones triggered by the stress response. All we need is to understand what our bodies are really doing and allow them to do it.

Crying is one of the ways that we release energy generated within our bodies. Recent research shows that a variety of chemicals are present in our tears depending on the reason that we're crying. This is huge. When crying is triggered by a stress response, our tears contain enkephalin, which is a natural painkiller that helps us process harmful experiences.

Yet look at the cultural messages we have around crying. Apparently it's only girls that cry (because we're awesome enough to not be afraid of our emotions!). In the United Kingdom we even have the idiom, *Keep a stiff upper lip*. This traditionally encouraged us not to show our emotions, because emotions and tears were considered a sign of weakness.

Like horses, we also process the energy of our stress response through movement. Think back to the very nature of the stress response. It's preparing us to fight or flee. That's why the horses tremble, move, and stomp their feet. We need to do the same. Yet again, movement like this has not been considered socially appropriate.

In the past in the United Kingdom, we had a belief that children should be seen and not heard. To some extent it still exists. That means that we were trained from birth to not respond naturally to our body's stress responses.

No wonder we have such a reputation for high alcohol consumption. It's traditionally been one of the few socially acceptable ways to process our stress responses.

The hormones from our stress responses affect our digestion. This means that it's normal to experience energy releasing from the stomach. An example of this is burping, which is something I do a lot when I release the energy of a stress response. Taken to the extreme, this is why some people actually vomit when processing emotional pain and limiting belief.

Sweating is a way of shifting energy within the body. It's why we sweat when we have a fever. The body is working to bring itself back into balance. If you have strong body odor, this is a sign that your body is releasing toxins, which are imbalances within the body, through your sweat.

Going to the toilet is a way of shifting energy within the body.

Making primal sounds is a way of releasing energy within the body.

Trembling and shaking is a way of releasing energy within the body.

Yawning is a way of releasing energy within the body.

The key to success in mastering your natural body is to become comfortable with what your body naturally does. Every involuntary function within your body is designed to bring your body back into a state of balance. When we stifle these functions, in accordance with societal beliefs about how we should act, we stifle our body's ability to stay in a state of balance and health.

Think about how the earth works. Whenever there is a build-up of pressure and tension, it causes the earth to shift its tectonic plates causing an earthquake. Or a volcano erupts. Or there's a tornado, or some other natural phenomenon. That's the earth bringing itself back into balance.

Your body functions in the same way. All you need to do is stop your mind getting in the way of your natural body and let your body do what it does best. We've been taught to fear our own bodily functions and treat them as if they were something to be embarrassed about rather than see them as wonderful mechanisms designed to help the body stay in balance.

Think about when you need to go to the toilet. You're desperate to relieve yourself. Your senses of pain and distress are activated. Your stomach feels full and uncomfortable.

Then you sit down and release. You've got to admit, it feels good. The elimination of waste brings your body back into balance.

Have you ever noticed that after a night of too much self-indulgence with alcohol, that when you have a bowel movement the next day you actually feel better?

Society tells us that we shouldn't really talk about stuff like this in polite society. Yet it's *not* talking about stuff like this that has contributed to people's ill health. If we don't talk about it then we don't know what's normal. If we don't normalize the way our bodies release energy, we experience shame and guilt towards ourselves. That is the biggest disconnect of all.

Body Awareness Guided Visualization

The following exercise is designed to help you reconnect to your natural body and strengthen your awareness of it. Take a moment and familiarize yourself with the exercise. If you want a recording of this exercise you can download one at: www.thenatureprocessonline.com/additionalresources.

Take a moment and get comfortable where you are sitting. Make sure your bum fills the seat and get your feet on the ground. It's important to make sure that you're relaxed and comfortable for this exercise.

If you need to, move your shoulders and stretch so that you can become fully comfortable.

Close your eyes, knowing that some of your natural senses will be activated as you do so.

Take a deep breath in. And a deep breath out. Take another deep breath in and another deep breath out.

The first thing that I want you to do is to activate your sense of memory and remember the nature experiences that you've had in the past. Think about being outside in your local area experiencing a sense of spaciousness; a sense of desire to connect; a sense of peace, tranquility, and silence.

Remember the emotions these senses created within you.

Acknowledge that in your mind you are there. Your body doesn't know the difference. Bring this awareness of nature fully into your mind and body.

Anchor yourself within these moments, to these experiences. Harness the sensory experience of nature. Know that you are safe and you are supported by nature, that nature is helping you to sense the nature within you.

Now start sensing your body. Start at the feet. Become aware of the pressure, that sense of pressure underneath your feet, the sense of contact and the sense of temperature. Are your feet hot? Are they cold?

As you move up into your legs, sense your legs and notice if there's any twitching. Sense your body and understand the way that your body wants to work. If you need to move, move.

Trust your body. Trust that your body knows exactly what you need.

Allow your senses to keep exploring up your thighs. If you're attracted to using your hands to help you sense your thighs, then do so. There's no right or wrong way to do this. There's only your way.

Keep on sensing that energy. Sense what is going on within your body for you.

Bring your awareness up through the groin area, up to the hips and the back. Pay attention. Do you have a feeling of balance or is there a feeling of stress? Is there tension? Is there something that needs to be moved? If you do, move. Trust your body to do exactly what you need in the moment.

Bring your awareness further up into the stomach, into the heart. If it helps you, imagine the heart pumping and beating all that blood around your body.

Stay focused on your sensory experience of your body. Are you able to stay present, without the mind become distracted?

Can you feel your body? As you keep on breathing, are you able to feel your lungs expanding and contracting? Is there movement within the stomach that supports this?

Observe what is going on through your wonderful fifty-four senses that allow you to experience your body in a new and different way.

Keep hold of your awareness and bring it up into the shoulders. Again, if you need to move, do it.

Feel your arms. Notice your sensory awareness. Move your arms right down to your fingers and if you want to move your fingers, feel the air surrounding your fingers as you do so. Can you feel this movement in you? The muscle moving underneath the skin?

Make a little movement with your fingers. Again, just keep all of the awareness of your fingers, your arms, your shoulders and neck. Remember that if you need to move, move. Your body knows exactly what it needs.

Ignore the mind. Focus on the senses. Bring your awareness up into the head.

Feel your whole body as you are just now from a state of loving. Respect the wisdom of your body. Your body is a wise beacon of knowledge on this physical plane. It deserves order and respect for its ability to be here as part of the earth, sensing itself.

Take a few moments to sit with whatever sensations are arising. If you get the urge to cough or make noises, let them out. Nobody else matters. There's only you present.

Give yourself a moment. Offer thanks to your body for the wisdom that it contains, for the natural wisdom, full of power and strength. Your body knows intuitively how to bring you back into balance.

Offer thanks, especially if you are suffering from any illnesses. Offer thanks to your body. Your body is not weak because it is ill; your body is the strongest it has ever been.

If you're suffering from an illness, your body is working twice as hard to work, to bring you back as much as it possibly can to a state of balance and wholeness. That is incredible. That is power. Feel this and give thanks.

When you're ready, open your eyes and re-engage with the world around you.

If you need to take a moment to reflect on your experience, do so. If you'd like to journal about your experience, get a paper and pen.

Connect to Your Natural Body

This is where you use your fifty-four senses to focus fully on your natural body. Instead of sensing nature outside of you, you're now sensing nature within. You don't have to be outside to sense your natural body, though I will talk about connecting your natural body to your natural presence at the end of this chapter.

You are with your body 100% of the time, yet many of us are so caught up in the Beta brainwave state that we disconnect from our bodies and the sensations within it. Take a moment and bring your awareness to your body right now. Is it comfortable or are there aches and pains present? If so, what are you attracted to doing?

As I type this, I'm conscious of tension in my shoulders. I went for a jog this morning and noticed that this helped release the tension in my shoulders from yesterday. Yet it's back. It's a sign that I'm spending too long at the computer and that my posture is not supportive of what I'm doing. Even after taking regular breaks to stretch and move my body, this tension is not going away.

Ideally I should be taking a longer break about now and doing some more movement. Yet my mind is fully engaged with what I'm writing and doesn't want to stop. This is a sign I'm currently more in my mind in a Beta brainwave state than present in my body.

To balance this I have to stop, stretch, and bring my awareness to include not only what I'm writing here for you but also how my body feels as I do it.

Honestly? My body wants to go and lie down on the earth outside and totally stretch!

I'm lucky. I'm my own boss, so I can choose whether to continue working or listen to my body. Not everyone has this luxury. What you need to do is balance this awareness of your natural body with your pre-existing modern day life commitments. Find a way to compromise. Currently I'm moving my body and stretching it as I type.

Remember what I said in the previous chapter. This is about finding a way to connect to nature, both within and without, in the midst of your daily life. This is where the true power of this process lies.

There's a huge connection between your body and the food that you put into it. An exploration of this is beyond the focus of this book.

However, a great time to focus on our natural body is when we eat. Pay attention to the sensations you experience as you eat your food. Notice the different sensations that arise in your body depending on what you eat. Are there foods that make you feel more energized? Happier? Or is what you're eating triggering your senses of pain, distress, and fear?

This is a huge factor within emotional eating. Again this goes beyond the focus of this book, yet I want to quickly address this issue because it's one that a lot of people struggle with. I've personally spent years exploring my natural body and its relationship to emotional eating.

Now the idea of connecting with your natural body is not about forcing change upon it, especially from a place of shame and guilt. This is what keeps a lot of emotional eaters trapped in a cycle of powerlessness around their food choices. If you're emotionally eating there's an underlying cause that needs to be dealt with first.

The most successful way I've found to treat my emotional eating is to observe that I'm doing it and experience the physical sensations that come from it, but not to force myself to stop doing it. Instead I come from a place of love and compassion. Right in that moment, this is the best coping mechanism that I have at hand.

When I removed the guilt and shame around my eating behavior, it became easier to address the underlying cause of why I was eating in the first place. Once I addressed that issue I no longer felt the attraction to emotionally eat.

This insight has totally transformed my relationship with food. Because I believed myself to be weak and powerless when it came to food, I was one of those people who would swing between emotionally eating and fasting as subconscious forms of punishment.

Now I trust my body to eat what it needs. If in a moment what it needs is a huge piece of cake or some other sugary processed food that we've been told we shouldn't eat, I let myself eat it. It's all about balance, not deprivation.

How to Adapt Your Natural Body to Physical Disability

During a recent Nature Process online session, one of the participants asked a question about how to adapt the exploration of the natural body, especially with regards to the Body Awareness Guided Visualization as she was a paraplegic and couldn't experience some of the things I mentioned in the exercise. The following is a guideline for anyone who has some form of physical disability.

You need to start with where you are and what you can already sense. Don't focus on what you *can't* sense; that's counterproductive to developing your natural body and will only lead to frustration. Remember from the last chapter that pain, distress, and fear are sensory signs that you need to engage other senses for your own well-being.

When you focus on what you can sense, follow that sensations as far as it goes. Then push your awareness further and see what other sensations you can notice.

Repeat and play with this process. Is it possible to expand your awareness of your natural body beyond what you currently sense?

To help you additionally explore your natural body, get a massage. This is a great way to tune into sensations and feelings in the body without having to make an effort. It's also got the added benefits of stimulating circulation, helping the nervous system to function more effectively, and relieving pain and muscle tension.

See if it's possible to get a massage out in nature. This will help you shift into the Theta brainwave state so that not only are you connected to nature but you'll also be able to tap into your body's wisdom. It will tell you how best to move and expand your natural body.

If you have a physical disability, it's even more important to connect with your natural body and learn to trust it. It will give you the best wisdom possible about what you're capable of sensing, experiencing, and doing.

The Body's Response to Emotions

There's a growing belief within society, supported by recent research, that specific body parts or ailments are actually connected to specific issues or emotions. On a basic level, all emotional responses are connected to the body through the stress response that I explained at the start of this chapter. If we do not fully process the stress hormones related to emotional pain and limiting beliefs, these chemicals stay trapped within our body. This belief is merely a further development of this basic physiological response.

Through working with my own ill health, I've found this approach to be particularly effective. By understanding what emotional issues could contribute to a specific health issue, I've been able to explore emotional pain and limiting beliefs that I've unconsciously held onto. As I worked with releasing these emotional issues, I found that my health improved.

Should you wish to explore this further for any particular health issue that you may have, a noted expert within this field is Louise Hay, founder of the publishing company Hay House, which is the biggest mind-body-spirit publishing house in the world.

In the 1980s Louise Hay wrote a book called *You Can Heal Your Life*, in which she explained how physical illness can have its roots in the way we think. This book has sold over thirty-five million copies worldwide, making her one of the largest selling women authors after J.K. Rowling, Danielle Steel, and Barbara Cartland, who all wrote fiction. That's a pretty impressive claim to fame!

The companion guide, *Heal Your Body*, offers an extensive list of ailments and their root mental causes, along with affirmations to change the way you think. I personally don't find the affirmations particularly helpful, but exploring the root causes of my asthma and eczema through her work was very useful for me in my own healing journey with my natural body.

To start exploring how emotional pain and limiting beliefs manifest in your body, stop and take a moment now to think about something that you are currently hurt and upset over, or something traumatic that happened to you in the past.

What sensations and feelings arise in the body as you do?

Pay attention to these, and then pay attention to how your body wants to move in response to your awareness of these sensations and feelings. That's your natural body looking to shift the stress response generated by these thoughts.

Connect Your Natural Body to Your Natural Presence

Once you've become aware of your natural body it's time to take it outside and fully connect it to your natural presence. It's not about doing exercise outside, though you can if you want to. It's about being able to maintain an awareness of both nature and your body, and trusting whatever you are inspired to do.

Too often when people exercise they're not really connected to their natural presence nor their natural body. This is when accidents and injuries occur.

Start from where you are in the moment. Maybe all you're attracted to doing is sitting outside. That's ok. If you want to walk, great, but don't force yourself. Let nature within and without guide you through this.

As you tap into your natural presence you're silencing your mind and becoming aware of nature. When you turn your focus and attention inwards, you connect nature outside of your body with the nature that is part of you.

Nature will start reducing stress and boosting your immune system on a physiological level. All you need to do is to pay attention to the sensations and feelings in your body as they arrive and move your body in a way that feels good.

This is only the first two parts of The Nature Process, and already you will be starting to shift energy around emotional pain and limiting beliefs. This is a great way to manage your stress levels and experience a deeper sense of relaxation.

If you experience a sudden illness, you can use these two parts of The Nature Process to jump-start your healing. In fact, this should be the first tool that you use. This can be a challenge because when we become suddenly ill it can trigger all sorts of pain, distress, and fear. Remember, these are signs that you need to reconnect to some of your other senses.

Maybe you're not attracted to going outside. That's ok. Remember that a nature view from a window has powerful healing effects. If you don't have access to a natural view, this is where you use the Body Awareness Guided Visualization in this book. You use your sense of memory to activate a previous nature experience that allows your body to sense that it is present in nature.

If your sense of concentration is weakened and you can't focus enough to do this, enlist the help of someone else. Share your nature memory with them and ask them to share their own nature memories with you.

Just like with your natural presence, the more you practice connecting your natural body and your natural presence, the easier it becomes. You're also training yourself to use this part of the process as your default response to stress and illness. By doing so you spend less time sensing pain, distress, and fear, and more time connected to nature within you and around you.

Chapter 5: Natural Attractions

Try and penetrate with our limited means the secrets of nature and you will find that, behind all the discernible concatenations, there remains something subtle, intangible and inexplicable.

- Albert Einstein

Dude, engage your fifty-four senses through your natural presence and natural body and connect them to natural attractions. Then you'll understand the secrets of nature much better!

- Tabitha Jayne

By now you should be engaging your fifty-four senses more and more as you experience your natural presence and your natural body. As you go deeper into The Nature Process it's easy to get lost in your exploration of nature and forget that the purpose of the process when it's experienced in its entirety is in fact to let go of emotional pain and limiting beliefs. That's ok.

You're learning through this process to experience a deeper relationship with nature than you've ever had before. That's something to get excited about. What you'll find out is that you can always go deeper into each part of the process. You're never going to get to the end and discover everything there is to know about each part. To me, this is one of the most attractive things about a conscious connection to nature.

Natural attractions is the pivotal part of the process. It will challenge you and excite you. It's also the part that will cause you at times to question what you're doing. Some of you will even find that this is as far as you'll allow yourself to go with The Nature Process at this moment in time. That's ok too.

It's important that you don't push any part of this process. It takes time to fully integrate into your psyche all the experiences you'll have with the first two parts of this process. If where you need to be is focusing only on fully experiencing the first three parts, then that's where you need to be. There is no right or wrong way to do this, only your way.

If you're attracted to experiencing The Nature Process in its entirety as quickly as possible, I suggest that you have the personal guidance of one of our trained Nature Process facilitators. Please email me at tabitha@tabithajayne.com for more information.

You'll know that you've mastered this part of the process when you live every second of your life from a place of connection to natural attractions. This is more challenging than it sounds, because this part of the process is where you start to come up against your deepest limiting beliefs.

The Importance of Following Your Natural Attractions

When we listen to and follow our natural attractions, we're following the wisdom that has existed within nature for 13.7 billion years—the dawn of our universe. Following our natural attractions allows us to exist in a beautiful dance with life, one that allows our emotional pain and limiting beliefs to be subsumed into nature so that we remain in a state of balance with ourselves and with the world.

This is the quickest way to bring balance back to our body, mind, and soul. Nature is fully balanced at all times. As soon as there is imbalance, action naturally occurs to restore equilibrium.

We see this truth reflected back to us in global warming and climate change. For every action taken by humanity that brings the planet out of balance there is a corresponding response to restore equilibrium. This is true even on a micro level. Until we understand that as individuals we must first master ourselves, the symptoms of global warming and climate change will continue to increase. It's nature's way to get our attention and communicate this message to us.

Our fifty-four senses are fundamental to both hearing this message and applying it to ourselves. Right now, within most of humanity our collective senses of pain, distress, and fear are fully activated but we don't know what to do with them. We need to activate the rest of our senses and allow natural attractions to bring us back into a state of total balance. It starts first on an individual level and then on a collective level.

I'll simplify natural attractions to ensure that you fully understand them:
1. Stop doing things that make you feel bad.
2. Start doing things that make you feel good.
3. Harm neither yourself nor others.

This is the cardinal rule of natural attractions. When you do more of what makes you feel good you are re-aligning yourself with the power of nature.

We have a collective belief that change and growth is difficult. It's only difficult when we stay in our senses of pain, distress, and fear then try to change and grow from there. When we activate the rest of our fifty-four senses and use them, change and growth become joyful, fun, and easy.

The challenge that we all have is that when we try to do things that make us feel good, we can feel guilty. Social and cultural conditioning from thousands of years of disconnection from nature sticks in our minds. How often have you stopped yourself from doing something that makes you feel good through a sense of obligation, guilt, or fear of upsetting a loved one? Your mind offers all these wonderful justifications of why you can't. This is nothing more than nature-disconnected bullshit. Sadly, too many of us listen to our mind and ignore our natural attractions.

It's important to note here that following our natural attractions is *not* about indulging in hedonism. Too often when people follow their hedonistic tendencies they end up hurting themselves and others. This clearly contravenes the third tenet of the principles of natural attraction. There is a difference between pursuing pleasure at all costs (which usually doesn't make people *really* feel good) and doing what intuitively makes you feel good. For example, if you feel ill, do you take time off work and allow yourself to rest, because that's what feels good, or do you force yourself to continue on as you consume a high dosage of medication to alleviate some of the pain you're experiencing just so that you don't lose out on earning money?

This is the part of The Nature Process that is going to challenge you the most. Our identity is so closely entwined with our beliefs that there is a fear of not knowing who we are without them. Our beliefs offer us a false sense of security, even if they keep us trapped in our senses of pain, distress, and fear. This can be so strong that we will argue to the contrary even when presented with alternative evidence. We will unconsciously lie to ourselves rather than trust our own senses and natural attractions.

If at any point you find yourself becoming angry or defensive or feel a desire to let people know you're right and justify it with your personal experience, then it's time to stop and celebrate. Natural attractions are showing you that there is something out of balance with who you truly are. You are not in your natural power at that moment.

The more you remember this, the more you will be able to follow natural attractions by activating your other senses. You will then spend less and less time in pain, fear and distress than you currently think is possible.

Learn About Natural Attractions from Cats

Cats are one of the most common pets in Europe and North America.

But as any cat owner will know, our feline friends like to remind us they're not fully domesticated.

The relationship between cats and humans goes back thousands of years. On the island of Cyprus, archaeological evidence from 9,500 years ago shows cats being used in burial rituals alongside humans. The ancient Egyptians viewed cats as sacred. Even causing the accidental death of one brought the death penalty.

The modern housecat descends from African wildcats and are cousins to other kinds of cats in the wild such as lions and tigers. One theory around how the domestication of cats happened is that rather than human domesticating cats, cats instead domesticated themselves. As humanity started civilizing itself, the collection of grain into storage increased the number of rodents. Cats moved in to take advantage of an easy food source. It was their choice to decide how much they wanted to integrate themselves with humans, not the other way around.

If you've ever had an opportunity to live with a cat you'll have seen that all they do is eat, play, and sleep. A far more powerful title for Elizabeth Gilbert's book, there. We can learn a lot from them.

If you've had the pleasure of being owned by a cat, you will have found yourself in the privileged position of giving them food and shelter, and accommodating all your cat's needs just so she can eat, play, and sleep. All without the guarantee that you'll get petting rights!

In each and every waking moment, a cat follows its natural attractions. It doesn't do anything that it doesn't want to, unless it's an enforced visit to the vet by us! A cat is able to exist in the present moment and live a life fully inspired by its natural attractions, even if they are indoor animals.

Yet the longer that they live with us, the weaker their natural attractions become. We have cats that are adopting human problems, like obesity and asthma, something that would never have happened in the wild. I'm aware that critics of this argument would point out some of the squalid conditions that cats have to endure. Those conditions exist because of humanity, not because other cats are holding onto the resources and depriving others of them, like we do with our fellow brothers and sisters.

Before civilization, we humans were like cats. Nature was our caregiver and enabled us to have an existence of eat, play, and sleep. There was a time in our history when food and water was freely provided by the earth, and when we were able to shelter ourselves without the need to pay rent to do so. This was a time of total abundance, one that we struggle today to understand as even possible for us.

History, which is always written by those who conquered others, wants us to believe that we're at the peak of human evolution, that it was worse for us in the past, and we should be lucky to live like we do today. If you go far enough back into our past, beyond the records of civilization, you'll find that this isn't true. People at that time were simply too busy fully experiencing this abundance of life to want to record it just in case those who came afterwards needed to be reminded about it!

As we established civilizations, we created systems and structures within society that started to disconnect us from our own natural attractions. There's an argument that it was the rise of industrialization in the early nineteenth century that led to humanity's disconnect from nature.

In reality, it's been a slow process that started over thirteen thousand years ago when there was a cataclysmic natural disaster of such epic proportions that destroyed the world as humans experienced it and their trust in nature along with it.

Although controversial, there's growing scientific evidence that supports the fact that a comet hit the earth all those years ago with signs of the impact being found in Mexico, Canada, United States, Russia, Syria, and parts of Europe.

Furthermore, over six hundred different cultures from around the world have stories within their mythology of a time when the sky darkened, the ocean boiled, and plants, animals, and humans began to die out.

Today we have middlemen—corporations and governments—that constrain our relationship to nature and base it upon a monetary system, something which doesn't exist in nature. If we want to access nature and its life-enhancing benefits, we need to pay. Humanity has created a system whereby we polluted so much of our natural resources that we need money to get access to clean drinking water and food. We need money to access adequate shelter, and if you don't have it you're forced to lived in poverty, deprived of basic human needs that nature was once able to provide for us.

No cats were attracted to doing that from their natural attractions. Seriously, which species is actually more intelligent?

Natural Attractions in Working Life

Think about your job. You probably spend up to forty hours a week working just to bring in the money you need to satisfy your basic human needs. Meanwhile, you feel frustrated that you're not spending enough time with your loved ones or being able to do what you really want with your life. There is no other animal on this planet that does this. Every other animal lives from their natural attractions.

I went outside and tried to think of an example that would contradict this but I couldn't find one. As I watched the ants scurry about industriously over the ground on whatever mission they were on I realized this wasn't work for them. It was merely what they were attracted to doing.

Furthermore, the ants don't have to drag their asses out of bed and into work just for the sake of earning some money to survive. They just get on with creating what is necessary, not just for themselves to thrive individually but for their whole ant colony, which could be comprised of millions of ants.

Ants are complex social insects that are able to organize themselves, modify their habitat, tap into natural resources, and defend themselves in such a way that it puts us humans to shame. They're so successful at what they do that it's been estimated that they comprise of up to twenty percent of the biomass of land animals.

The most interesting part of the organization of an ant colony is that not all the females reproduce. This is left up to the queen ants of the colony. Now we might think of them as the leaders of the colony, which is not strictly true. The authority and decision-making processes lie with each and every individual ant that is part of the colony.

Queen ants are the only ants to have wings. They need them to reproduce and start a successful colony. In this way they are leaders. After reproduction, the queen ants either detach their own wings or let the worker ants in their colony chew them off.

Think about this in comparison to the leaders we currently have at work and in government. How many of them truly put the good of their people first?

Natural Attraction in Exercise

Think about cats again for a minute. Unless you overfeed them, they naturally maintain a sleek and healthy body. You don't see the cat setting an alarm to get up and go exercise at five o'clock in the morning before it goes to work. You don't see it counting how many times it's jumped up to try to get the fly that's buzzing around.

A cat doesn't even make an effort to exercise. When a cat feels attracted to moving its body, it does. This is the play part of eat, play, and sleep. Sadly for most cat owners, this is usually high-energy running around the house in the early hours of the morning. Or catching mice and rats and then waking you up as they throw them around your bedroom in joy before offering them to you as a token of their affection.

Cats in general are able to stay fit and healthy without excess fat with no effort at all. In contrast, we humans struggle to stay fit and healthy, and obesity is a rising epidemic. The fitness industry in the United Kingdom alone was worth £3.92 billion in 2013. That's a lot of people going to the gym instead of just getting outside, having fun in nature, and playing when they're inspired to do so.

As I sit here with a cat on my lap that is emitting noxious gases from its rear end while I develop an ache in my shoulders from hunching over the laptop as I deliberately try not to disturb its slumber, I ask you again, which species is the most intelligent?

The Insanity of Civilization

We've created a society that is damaging our personal, social, and environmental well-being. If you pop on over to Wikipedia, the online go-to source for everything you want to know about anything, you'll find that a key element of civilization is its perceived separation from and domination over the natural environment.

In his incredible book *Endgame, Vol 1,* Derrick Jensen presents an awesome analysis of the insanity of civilization. He makes the observation that the real reason both the Egyptian and Roman civilizations ended was because they consumed too many of the available natural resources in their respective regions and were unable to maintain their growth and expansion.

There's a lesson in this for us with the current state of our own modern civilization, which derives many of our beliefs and attitudes from these extinct civilizations. Einstein allegedly defined insanity as doing the same thing over and over again but expecting different results. This quote has never been more relevant than it is when it comes to our civilized behavior.

If we don't change both our individual and collective behavior, then its highly likely that we'll be going the way of the dodo. And just like it was human behavior that was directly responsible for the dodo's extinction, we'll have no one to blame for it but ourselves.

You need to understand that I'm not asking you to destroy civilization and go back to living a life in nature devoid of all the wonderful comforts we've developed that make our life easier. After spending time in nature contemplating this and releasing my own limiting beliefs on this topic with the support of The Nature Process, I truly don't believe that we need to. What I'm asking you to do is question which of these comforts are truly necessary and make a conscious choice about what parts of civilization you want to support.

I love technology. That's why I call myself a nature geek. The internet allows me to sit here in the middle of the French countryside and write this book, and then share it with people all over the world. That's awesome. Airplanes allow me to travel from one part of the world to another in a day. I freaking love that. Applications such as Skype allow me to connect with people all over the world without even leaving my home. I get to stay in touch with my friends and family while I fulfill my natural attraction to travel and experience a conscious connection with the land all over planet earth. Seriously? There's nothing better than making silly faces at my nieces on the webcam while knowing that I'm going to be able to hug them again soon.

But a huge wardrobe filled with the latest fashion made at the expense of human and the planet's well-being? That makes no sense to me.

Pretending to own my own property with a mortgage that makes the bank rich and filling the space with lots of stuff that I've bought from slaving my guts out for forty hours a week? Been there, done that, then sold my flat so that I could publish my first book and spend three months traveling in Canada and the United States.

Having someone else dictate how much time I can spend on my greatest passions in life? You've got to be kidding me.

Dying with all my dreams unfulfilled just because they contradict the expectations of our current social norms? Hell no.

Just like that annoying child who never shuts up and keeps on asking why, I've questioned everything about the civilization in which we live, right down to the most commonly accepted practices.

Especially when it comes to women.

Put Those Heels Away

Even though I've always preferred bare feet, I used to be one of those women who were proud to say that they could run in high heels. Now 99.99% of the time I wear barefoot shoes or am actually barefoot, and have done so for years.

The turning point for me was when I read that 80% of foot problems are caused by badly fitting shoes. Modern footwear has evolved to weaken the sensory experiences we can have through our feet.

When I researched further, especially into high heels, I discovered that while the benefits to wearing them are only aesthetic, the list of health problems they cause is quite severe.

It got me thinking, Why do women wear high heels? There's a learned belief we have that high heels are sexy and erotic. They've become a symbol of the western women's femininity. Why is that so many women are prepared to damage their feet in the name of beauty? What's sexy about bunions and corns?

At the same time as we Western women are voluntarily destroying our own feet through wearing high heels, we react in horror at the ancient Chinese custom of foot binding (thankfully not done now). This is where the woman's feet were tightly bound and in some cases the bones actually broken because women were considered more attractive with dainty feet.

We don't realize that high heels are our modern version of this. If you go back into the history of high heels, you'll find that high heels were originally developed in the ninth century CE to help horse riders keep their feet in the stirrups. It was also very common for men to wear high heels, too, in the past.

Forget About The Bra

While we women have been playing with our breasts (pun intended!) for thousands of years, the modern bra is a fairly recent development. Within the last one hundred years, they've become such a cultural norm that a woman who chooses not to wear a bra can be severely criticized, especially in our celebrity body-bashing culture.

We're told that it's necessary for us to wear a bra because it supports our breast muscles and gives them better shape (note the aesthetic value coming in here again?).

Yet research is now showing that wearing bras can affect the functioning of the lymph nodes in our breasts, potentially leading to breast cancer. In indigenous cultures where bra wearing is rare, apparently so is breast cancer.

More research shows that if we don't wear a bra, our breasts naturally develop muscles that help keep them naturally perky.

If you're a woman reading this, stop for a moment and think about all the beliefs you have around wearing a bra. Then think about how good it feels when you take it off at the end of the day. If you're a man, think about how good breasts feel when they're not in bras, especially the padded kind.

I'm not encouraging you to immediately run out, burn your bras, and liberate your breasts. If you feel good wearing a bra, then keep wearing one. I merely want you to consider the possibility that some things we accept without question are not necessarily the best things for us and our bodies.

If humanity has been wrong about something as seemingly insignificant as high heels and bras, then what else have we been wrong about?

Natural Attractions and Growth

What we label "death" nature calls transformation and growth. If you don't believe me I challenge you to go out into nature and find an example of death. You won't be able to.

When a tree "dies," it transforms into a source of new life. Fungi grows on it. Insects and animals make their home in it.

When an animal "dies," its body decays and become a food source for other animals. Unless, of course, you're a human animal, because ever since the rise of civilization we've just pumped your body full of toxic chemicals to preserve you, stuck you in a box, and kept you fundamentally disconnected from nature even in death.

You might remember from the introduction that when we scattered my brother's ashes in the forest, small red flowers sprung up everywhere they'd touched the earth. Witnessing that was the start of my perspective shift into realizing that not only do I connect to myself out in nature, but I also connect to my brother.

This understanding of growth has fundamentally shifted my perspective on death and grief so much so that I can't relate to how most people experience death and grief anymore. It was one of the reasons that I knew

I had to walk away from working solely in this area. Most people in the early stages of grief aren't able to consider a different perspective. Some people are never able to consider a different perspective and stay stuck in grief their whole life.

This is compounded by the language that we use around this topic. We tell people that we've lost a loved one. We don't lose our loved ones after death. If you choose to let them, they remain just as much a part of our lives as they did when they were alive.

Relationships don't end just because people die. They continue on in our hearts and minds. It's just that the relationship has transformed and grown into a different one.

We talk about missing our loved one. I don't miss my brother. That would mean that I notice the absence of his presence in my life. Over the last twelve years, I've worked hard on the relationship with my brother to ensure that he is present in everything I do. He's still here. He's just in a different form than before.

Remember the definition of natural attractions from chapter two: Natural attractions are the space that exists between atoms and particles, and the pull that brings them together to create solid objects.

As I mentioned in the first chapter, quantum mechanics shows that when two particles have had a physical connection, this connection never dies. Even if the particles are separated, a change in one particle causes a change in the other. Once you've been physically connected to someone, you're always connected to them.

This is natural attractions at its finest.

Find the Blocks in Your Natural Attractions

As I mentioned at the start of this chapter, this is the part of The Nature Process that is going to help you uncover all the lovely hidden beliefs that are stopping you from accessing your natural power.

I've deliberately chosen the topics that I talked about in this chapter to help you see where some of your limiting beliefs lie and so that you can start questioning yourself about everything you believe in.

Pay attention to your thoughts about not just the topics covered here but with regards to everything you believe to be true. What you'll notice is that small unconscious limiting beliefs will arise, which you'll be able to change without any effort.

This is because you have no attachment to them. They're not really that important to you and how you see yourself as a person.

The beliefs that cause the strongest emotional response that doesn't feel good within you are the ones that not only contribute to your emotional pain but also prevent you from stepping fully into your natural power.

All you need to do at this stage is make a note of them either mentally or physically. You don't need to go into them and spend time trying to figure out where the belief has come from. That's you just getting caught up in the story that reinforces the belief.

When you put all five stages of The Nature Process together, you remove these beliefs on a sensory level, which allows you to bypass the old story and allow a new, empowering one to emerge.

This is where we get stuck when it comes to trying to let go of deep emotional pain and limiting beliefs. We believe that we need to share our story, and go over it again and again to make sense of it. What we're actually doing here is reinforcing the pain, distress, and fear that the emotional pain is triggering. To borrow a phrase from the Scottish comedy show *Chewin' the Fat*, "Gonnae no dae that."

Seriously. Stop telling the same old story that makes you feel bad when you do. Start following your natural attractions and find something else to do that is going to make you feel better.

Connect Your Natural Attractions to Nature

So far, this chapter has been a general explanation of natural attractions and how our disconnect from them affects our entire lives. Now you need to understand how you use natural attractions as part of The Nature Process.

The easiest way to do this right now so that you fully grasp this part is to go and find some nature, even if it's just an image on your computer for the moment.

Look at nature and let a specific part of it attract you. Don't let your mind get in the way by starting to question how to do this. Go with your first choice.

When you're outside this might not even be something that you notice through your eyes. If you're attracted to the sound of a bird's song or the sound of running water, that's ok too. Maybe it's even the feel of the earth under your feet or the tree bark as you touch it with your hand. Trust in whatever natural attraction you feel pulled towards and experience it through all of your senses.

As an example, I'm sitting here and looking out through the open patio doors into the garden. While there are many beautiful things to look at, I keep coming back to the red blossoms of a flowering plant that is resting in a potplant on a ledge in the stone wall.

Right now I don't know why. I don't need to. As I focus on them I become aware of different senses activating to make them stand out from everything else and keep my attention.

In this moment, natural attractions are at play. Whatever I need, in this moment, to bring myself back into balance is reflected in these red flowers.

Once you have this connection to nature through natural attractions, you need to stop and ask yourself why you like what you are attracted to.

For me, I like the red flowers on this plant because they are beautiful, bright, and outside.

Don't over-think this. Just allow whatever comes into your mind.

Once you have established your response, you then change the sentence from liking the red flowers to liking *yourself*.

I like myself because I am beautiful, bright, and outside.

Nature is reflecting back to me my own beauty and brightness.

I hope that I've captured the essence of this in my writing! The outside aspect puzzles me initially, because I'm inside as I type this. As I take a moment to think about this, using my sense of reason, I realize that this reflects the part of me that needs to be outside.

I've spent most of today inside. I've had a rather long cat nap that took up the whole afternoon, even after I got up late. It was raining earlier and after the storm knocked out the electricity I had to spend time figuring out how to switch everything back on. Not easy when you're in someone else's house; you don't know where everything is and you can't speak enough French to understand what the neighbors are saying as they try to help you!

I become aware of a tightness in the right part of my head. This tightness happens whenever I've spent too much time away from a conscious connection to nature.

It becomes clear. "I like myself because I'm outside" means that it's time for me to go for a nature adventure.

Now I'm not working with any emotional pain or limiting beliefs here. When you do this process with the intention of letting go of emotional pain and limiting beliefs, you'll have a starting point to anchor this part of the process specifically to them. I'll explain more about that when we get to the chapter that deals with putting the whole process together.

In the meantime, just enjoy discovering the truth of who you truly are through your natural attractions. On that note, I'm off outside!

Integrate Natural Attractions Into The Nature Process

It's important to realize that as you work on understanding each part of The Nature Process independently, you're not intentionally working on letting go of any emotional pain and limiting beliefs as of yet. It may happen naturally as you explore each part of the process. In fact it's nearly impossible for you *not* to experience any benefits as you go through each chapter and explore them experientially.

To build upon what you've already experienced in the previous chapters, you need to go outside. First take the time necessary to fully engage your natural presence. If you've been busy in the Beta brainwave state, this may take some time.

As I went outside after finishing the last section I started to run. Yet I wasn't fully present to nature. My mind was focused on writing this book and what I would say next to you, along with how much longer it would take to finish writing this chapter. It took me at least ten minutes to properly engage with my natural presence.

I sensed the different shades of green in the leaves of the trees, and the grey clouds that were left over from the storm highlighted by the red of the setting sun. I sensed the coolness of the air and the stillness of the evening. I sensed the silence of the cicadas, who normally chirped throughout the day, and saw the shimmering trails of the snails on the road.

Once you are conscious of your mind becoming quieter, which signifies that you are entering the Theta brainwave state, turn your senses inwards and focus on your natural body.

As I did this I noticed that I was breathing hard through my mouth because my running pace was too fast. I sensed pressure and strain in some muscles and the pounding of my heart and sweat coated my skin. I slowed down and started to pace myself and consciously breathe through my nose.

My natural presence slipped slightly as thoughts of whether or not I'd be able to continue entered my mind. I didn't engage with these thoughts. Instead I continued to deepen my natural presence by focusing on the nature around me, along with how my body felt as I continued to move it.

I spent the majority of my jog staying just with these two parts of The Nature Process. That was all I needed in the moment. Once both my natural presence and natural body were activated, at any moment I could have consciously chosen to bring natural attractions into this.

As you build up your experiential understanding, you'll want to go into your natural attractions again and again. As you go further into The Nature Process within the next two chapters, it will become second nature to you.

Then as I was nearing home, the mist attracted my senses. I stopped and allowed my natural presence to experience this. My natural body felt still and at peace. Natural attractions called me to go deeper into the mist.

I liked the mist because it lay close to the trees and brought a sense of mystery and magic to the land. This makes me smile.

I like myself because I lie close to the trees and bring a sense of mystery and magic to the land. Whenever I'm outside, I try to lie close to the trees. It's one of my favorite past times. Then I engage all of my senses and witness the depth and power of nature. It is through this conscious connection to nature that its mystery and magic comes to life.

The beauty of this is that if it's true for me, then it can also be true for you.

Natural attractions connect all of us together. They spin out from me, through this book, to you. We are one.

You too can lie close to the trees and bring a sense of mystery and magic to the land.

That's a glimpse of your natural power. A glimpse of the nature of who you truly are. Now get outside and experience it for yourself.

Chapter 6: Natural Communication

I speak to everyone in the same way, whether he is the garbage man or the president of the university.

- Albert Einstein

We've been taught to treat other humans in the same way, but when it comes to nature there's a huge block. How often have you spoken to nature in the same way that you speak towards another human being? This chapter teaches you exactly how to do that both as part of The Nature Process and by itself.

It's the thought of natural communication, especially with animals, that initially attracts people to exploring nature in a different way. It's also the part of the process that makes the most impact in the early stages. In fact it's likely that you've already experienced some form of natural communication already, whether you've acknowledged this or not.

Natural communication is the fun part of the process. We've all grown up with the story of Doctor Doolittle and secretly thought how cool it'd be to be like that. Natural communication allows you to experience nature as you've never experienced it before. It's also the part that makes your connection with nature fully conscious.

This is the start of integrating your mind with nature's wisdom so that you too can think and act from a place of balance and wholeness. It's where you start to explore how we live as humans from a totally different perspective.

Within The Nature Process, this is the part that amplifies the natural healing and balance effect of the earth and allows you to be fully supported by nature as you let go of any emotional pain and limiting beliefs that are stopping you from being fully in your natural power.

You'll know that you've mastered this part of the process when you find it easy and effortless to receive communication from nature, even when you're not consciously applying the process. As part of this you'll have developed your own unique way of blending all your senses together that allows you to translate nature's non-verbal communication into words.

The Gaia Hypothesis

This hypothesis was developed in the 1970s by an English independent scientist named James Lovelock, who was naturally attracted to this work through the longs walks out in nature he took when he was a child.

He proposed that the earth, along with the differing spheres surrounding it, is a self-regulating complex system where the earth and its organisms intelligently interact with each other through homeostasis to keep the earth in balance and capable of sustaining life.

There is a dynamic interplay between many processes on the earth's surface that help regulate surface temperature, atmosphere composition, and ocean salinity that's powered changes in the heat and temperature of the earth. This process actively ensures that optimal conditions for life remain on earth even when threatened by terrestrial or external events.

When we look at the earth as a self-regulating organism, we learn that we do not live *on* the earth but *in* the earth, as its atmosphere extends out four hundred kilometres above where we live on the surface. This is a small distinction but it's an important one.

The preposition "on" signifies contact. The preposition "in" signifies that we are contained by the limits of the earth. We are not merely connected to the earth through contact with its surface. We are part of it. If the earth is communicating with itself to bring itself back into balance, it must be communicating with us too because we are part of it.

Natural communication is our birthright. It's something that is natural and normal. We all possess this ability. The only reason we're not fully using it is because our social and cultural conditioning as discussed in the last chapter has trained us out of it.

This hypothesis demonstrates exactly how The Nature Process works both for the earth and for us. It's changes in chemical compositions that help the planet to remain in balance. You'll remember from chapter four that our emotional pain and limiting beliefs are nothing more than hormonal imbalances in our body triggered by the stress response. It's the dissolution of these hormones that bring us back into balance. It's the same process for the earth.

It's important to address quickly the debates about how much sentience, awareness, and consciousness the earth actually has. Lovelock stated that the processes that keep the earth in balance are unconscious. In contrast, *we* need to be fully conscious of this process in order for it to work. This is the first fundamental difference.

The second is that the earth doesn't experience human emotions. While it can experience pain, distress, and fear, it self-corrects so rapidly that it puts us to shame. It knows no shame, guilt, duty or obligation. Anything that has been created by civilization doesn't exist in the earth's consciousness.

Tilly Smith: Tsunami Heroine

Tilly Smith offers us a wonderful example of natural communication. She's not well known, yet her story demonstrates what happens when you're able to tap into your senses and recognize the communication of the earth for what it is.

The interpretation of her story as I tell it is not the commonly held version. Her story as it was portrayed in the media was an example of why education is so important. While this is true, it's also an example of the power of tapping into natural communication with the earth.

In 2004, Tilly and her family were on holiday in Thailand. At the time, Tilly was only ten years old. This is only a few years after children start shifting out of the Theta brainwave state, which means it's still easier for children of this age to drop into the Theta brainwave state than adults.

Two weeks before Tilly went on holiday, she had a lesson at school that had taught her all about tsunamis.

On the morning of the great Indian Ocean tsunami that killed over 230,000 people in fourteen countries, making it the biggest natural disaster in the recorded history of humanity, Tilly stood and looked out at the sea. Through her senses she noticed that the water had gone bubbly and frosty like beer as it started to recede. Her sense of memory was activated and through her sense of reason and logic she was able to correctly interpret what was about to happen.

Because she knew what was coming and the implication of it, this activated her senses of distress and fear. She told her mum, but at first her mum didn't listen to her as she was too busy reading a book. Yet Tilly didn't back down. Her sense of distress and fear was too strong and she was still too young for the societal and cultural conditioning that we experience to override it. The more she was ignored, the more hysterical she became.

Finally her dad listened to her and went to tell the hotel security. They evacuated the beach.

This beach was one of the few beaches along the stretch of the coastline that had no deaths. It's estimated that Tilly's actions saved the lives of over one hundred people. I have tears in my eyes just writing this because every time I share this story it moves me so much.

What makes this story even more compelling is that there was also research done into animal behavior at the time of the tsunami. One thing that was conspicuously absent as rescue workers were going through all the devastation left after the tsunami were the dead bodies of any animals.

As animals are more closely connected to the earth than us, they were able to tune into the earth's communication that something terrible was about to happen. They started fleeing for higher ground to get out of harm's way. They probably didn't even know what they were fleeing. They just trusted their sensory nature that told them to run. In contrast, as the waves receded on many beaches and left fish flopping about on the sand, many humans went towards the water. They took photos of the fish and sea. If you go and look at some of the recorded footage from the tsunami on YouTube, you'll see humans just standing on the beach watching the tsunami race towards them, unaware of their impending death. You'll even hear the disbelief and horror of the people recording this as they watch them swept away.

Tilly's story is a powerful testament of what's possible when we trust our senses and pay attention to the Earth's communication. The death toll of the tsunami is a powerful testament of what happens when we don't.

How to Communicate With Nature

As you might have guessed from the way I told Tilly's story, we communicate with nature through our fifty-four senses. That's why they are so imperative, and why I offered an in-depth explanation of them in chapter three. Many people only use the psychic sense to communicate with nature, and by doing so they miss a wealth of additional information.

When you're in the Theta brainwave state and you're using your fifty-four senses to connect and listen to nature's communication, it's like you switch on a universal translator. For those of you who aren't *Star Trek* fans and don't get the reference, a universal translator is a little piece of technology that can translate any language into the one you speak.

If you activate your universal translator by being in a deep Theta brainwave state and allowing all your senses to bring you information, you may find that you translate the information so rapidly into your native language that it seems like nature is really speaking to you in a verbal sense.

One of the keys to help you integrate this non-verbal communication is through deep listening to all your senses as they provide you with information. What this means is that you listen without trying to control or judge what you are experiencing. When applied to verbal communication, it also means listening to what's not being said along what is being said.

The beauty of deep listening is that you don't need to start practicing this in nature. You can practice it in any communication. The next time you're speaking with someone, make a conscious decision to listen more than you speak. If you're naturally introverted you'll find this very easy!

The second key is trust. When you enter a Theta mind state you are in essence entering into an altered state of consciousness. You process things differently. Your experience of time is different. Even your sense of space is different.

As you leave the Theta mind state and re-enter the Beta mind state, it's easy to discount what you've experienced and put it down to your imagination. You can start to question what happened and doubt that it was real.

The problem here is that when you doubt what you experience, you weaken your trust in what's happened. This then makes it harder for you to go back and communicate with nature. Trust is like a muscle. The more you exercise it, the stronger it gets.

What you hear from nature is never wrong. It's just that sometimes you haven't activated your universal translator properly so that what you get is distorted. If you have never done this before, it's very likely that your universal translator is not going to be working at one hundred percent. Just keep trusting what you get anyway. As you do you'll be able to fine tune the frequency.

Sometimes you may receive the message, but it takes your universal translator a little while to understand the communication. For example, I've just got off Skype with a friend. As we were chatting I noticed a little insect on the ground. As I looked closer at it, it jumped up onto the coffee table in front of me. As I chased it away I noticed its beautiful golden color and thought that it looked like a small cockroach.

I didn't think anything more of this until it jumped back up onto the table and started crawling over the television remote control. I interrupted my friend to tell her about this insect. As I did I felt an attraction to go onto Google and do a search for a golden cockroach.

Turns out my little friend is what's known as a tawny cockroach, and is actually not a pest but an important part of the ecosystem. Tawny cockroaches prefer to live outside in woodlands and don't like to co-habit with humans.

All of this might seem insignificant to you until you understand the deeper story behind this. When I arrived back in Scotland, another cockroach jumped out of my computer bag. My mum and grandmother wanted to kill it but I couldn't let them. Instead I saved him and created a small home for him in a terrarium.

Yet he was unhappy. I sensed that he'd rather be squished than live alone. As I did more research on cockroaches I found out that they were actually very social animals. I couldn't release him in Scotland as there's no known cockroaches in the area and I didn't want to create a potential ecological imbalance. Instead I promised him that I would take him to France and release him when I arrived, figuring that Spain and France must share cockroaches.

The day I arrived in France I did exactly this. However, a part of me was worried that Roachie, as I named him, would be ok. I didn't know if there were other cockroaches around. As I did all this research my universal translator finally kicked in. This other cockroach had come to let me know that Roachie was ok and had found friends. When I turned around to look again for him, he'd gone.

It might be easy for you in your Beta brainwave state right now to laugh at this and think I'm a bit insane. That's why you need to get out and experience your own natural communication. Then you'll know I'm not.

The last key you need to do this is to consciously integrate yourself into communication with whatever part of nature your natural attractions drew you to. You do this by asking permission.

Get Permission to Connect to Nature

Permission is a very simple concept, yet it's something that is misused and misunderstood again and again. One of the most common misconceptions is that once you get permission, you don't need to ask for it again.

Look at it from the perspective of being in a sexual relationship with someone. Just because they've given their consent once to having sex with you doesn't automatically mean they give consent for you to have sex with them whenever you want.

Nature is in a constant state of change, just like us. Just because you got permission in the past from a part of nature or a place to connect doesn't mean that you'll always have permission. Always take the time to check in and ask.

I learned this lesson myself when I returned to the Galician countryside. Behind my ex-partner's family house in the middle of nowhere is a beautiful forested mountain with old ruins at the top. I spent a lot of my time up the mountain experiencing my coursework for my Masters in Applied Ecopsychology. I have so many wonderful joyous moments in my memory from there—following wild horses up to the windmills, standing on a rock and breathing in the essence of the trees, discovering a natural altar and creating my own ritual there, and standing naked in the mist as it slowly fell and turned everything around me to dense white. I returned a year later after the end of my relationship. Excitedly I began walking up the mountain. As I did I threw open my senses and shouted internally, "Here I come!", which was my variation of not quite asking for permission but still connecting. I assumed I had consent so I didn't ask for it.

Immediately I felt as if a wall had been put up in front of me. Confused, I stopped and then I heard very clearly in my mind, "You're not welcome anymore." To tell you the truth, I was devastated. In fact I thought that I'd heard wrong, but I hadn't.

As I sensed more and more into the mountain's communication I was told that if I went back up the mountain it would undervalue all the previous experiences I'd had up there. I could have ignored that and continued, but I didn't. Instead I turned around, headed in the opposite direction, found a grove of trees and sobbed my heart out.

Getting permission helps you to set an energetic boundary as a way of helping you to acknowledge the difference between merely being present in nature and being consciously connected. As you experiment with the permission exercise below, you'll be able to recognize the difference.

When you ask for permission you can do it out aloud or silently. The choice is yours. It's not important how you do it, just that you do.

Also be aware that you might get consent from one part of nature but not another. For example, one time I was out and was attracted to climbing a tree. The tree was quite happy for me to do this but the bunches of nettles around the tree trunk weren't. I sensed them say that if I could climb the tree without stepping on them I could have permission. When I looked I saw that this wasn't possible. Needless to say I didn't climb the tree after all!

The Permission Exercise

The following instructions are adapted from Dr. Mike's book, *Reconnecting with Nature: Finding Wellness through Restoring Your Bond with the Earth*. They're the same instructions that I send to my private clients so that they would have a guideline to remind them of how to get permission from nature.

Go to something in nature that you find attractive. Some suggestions are a park, a backyard, an aquarium, or even a potted plant.

When you get to it, notice how you feel. Are you able to offer thanks for any good feelings you may have?

Treat this area fairly as you would with a friend or equal. Ask permission for you to visit, enjoy and learn from this natural area.

Doing this increases your sensitivity to the area. Ask it if it will help you learn from it. Learning from it can't take place if there is a lack of safety and the potential for injury and destruction, either from it or you.

Wait for half a minute. Look for signs of danger such as thorns, bees, cliff faces, etc. If the area still feels attractive, or becomes more attractive, you have gained its consent.

If this portion of the natural area you visit no longer feels attractive, simply select another natural part that attracts you and repeat this process.

That's it. It's this simple. What's powerful about this exercise is that you can bring it into your daily life with every human encounter you have so that this becomes a natural and instinctive way to start any form of communication. Don't underestimate the power of this. It will revolutionize your relationships. Try it and see for yourself.

When you pay attention to consent in human communication, you'll find that a large amount of communication between us all is actually non-consensual. We automatically assume that people want (or need!) to listen to us and can get offended when they don't. Think about the number of times that you've gotten annoyed because someone isn't listening to you. Did you ask for their permission first?

How to Know You've Gotten Consent

It's easy to know if you get consent from another human being. All they need to do is to let you know with words. Nature has no words. Its consent is non-verbal.

As I developed The Nature Process I realized that understanding this consent can be difficult for people at first. Quite a few people were surprised to see what their experience of consent was when I personally guided them through The Nature Process. They were expecting something more. Sometimes consent can be nothing more than a subtle shift in your senses that is easy to override and doubt.

One of the participants in The Nature Process online community (If you want to join the facebook group go to: http://www.facebook.com/groups/naturalecosystem) shared that she was having difficulty in knowing whether she had gained consent or not, and believed that she wasn't capable of sensing it.

I asked her to go out into nature, take herself through The Nature Process, and then come back and share what had happened with the community.

She told us that it was a beautiful morning in the bush. She stopped at a large gum tree that attracted her, from the same family as the one near her house. It was such a beautiful tree. At this time of year, the bark peels off the trunk in long strips. These strips catch on the branches below and reveal the smoothness of the white bark beneath. The rising sun was reflecting on the high branches.

She couldn't register much sensations in her body but she noticed a kind of warmth around her heart. As there wasn't much happening she kept on drifting back into the mind and getting lost in her thoughts. She noticed how much her mind had developed at the expense of her senses.

Two things need to be pointed out here.

Number one, if you keep drifting back into your mind, then this is a sign that you need to develop your natural presence more. I remember how I felt after doing the introductory webinar for The Nature Process online. My mind was already very active after travelling back up from London earlier that day. The technological experience of the webinar overwhelmed me so much that as I walked to my sister's house, which was twenty minutes away, I couldn't fully sink into natural presence. My mind was still distracting me. It took a conversation with my sister, another twenty-minute walk and the darkness and solitude of the local golf course at night before I could fully sink back into the Theta brainwave state. It was only then that I could nature-process the stuff that had come up for me as a result of the webinar.

Number two, the warmth this participant experienced in her heart was a sign of consent. It was the most she was capable of experiencing in that moment because she wasn't fully in her natural presence. This raises an important point here. Many of us unintentionally want to rush ahead, find the natural attraction, and connect with it so that we can let go of our emotional pain and limiting beliefs and get on with our life. We're impatient. This is a human trait that will interrupt your experience of The Nature Process.

Lao Tzu, a philosopher and poet of ancient China, said it best: "Nature does not hurry, yet everything is accomplished."

It may take up to a minute before you sense signs that you have nature's consent. Take your phone out and set a minute on the timer. Close your eyes and wait. You'll find that this minute seems so long.

In today's busy, modern world we've come to expect instant responses through text messages and email. Nature doesn't work like this. You have to give it time to get your answer.

Remember the key lesson from natural attractions and apply it here. If you feel the goodness of nature in any way, you have consent. If you don't feel the goodness, you don't have consent.

Another participant shared how she was in the woods during the week. As she walked through them she felt attracted to touching several tress and said to each one, "Hello, how are you doing?" As she did she sensed a soft flow of energy coming back at her but she didn't know what it meant. That again was consent, and the start of non-verbal communication, specifically here with trees.

Once you recognize what consent feels like, you can deepen your understanding of it. You can also experiment with this part of The Nature Process on its own. If your goal is merely to understand natural communication better, then you don't need to do the other parts of the process first.

Engaging in Natural Communication

Start by asking yes/no questions, as it's easier to understand the responses. This will help build up your confidence and make you comfortable.

I remember a few years ago when I was experimenting with my cat Fwit, who now lives with my mum. I was working on exploring telepathic communication with animals, which I'll address fully in the next section of the book. As I sat on the bed with Fwit sitting in front of me, I wasn't sure if I was connecting with her or not. I stared into her eyes, and rather than asking, I projected frustratedly, "I wish you would blink your eyes to give me a sign if I was connecting with you or not!"

No sooner had the thought been created in my mind than Fwit, who had been staring at me in that really unnerving unblinking-cat way, blinked her eyes. I was so shocked and surprised by this that my connection to her dropped. My brain wasn't sure whether to believe that this really was a sign or just wishful thinking! For some reason it was easier for me to accept that I could communicate with trees than with animals. A great example of a hidden limiting belief being fully illuminated there!

Once you have the confidence that you are actually engaging in communication, you can then explore open-ended questions. In order to translate the answers to these you need to be fully focused on your senses and be aware of which ones are being activated. For example, a memory might come to mind or you'll feel attracted to moving your body in a certain way. It's important to go with whatever comes up, even if you don't initially understand it.

Pay attention to where your eyes are drawn and what sounds you hear. Maybe there will be a gust of wind or raindrops will start to fall. In the moment when you're engaged with natural communication, everything that happens that you sense is significant.

It can also be helpful to start a dialogue with yourself using your sense of language. This can make it easier for you to get your universal translator fully working. Ask a question and then give yourself the answer based on what you're sensing.

Once you're comfortable with this you can add another layer onto The Nature Process; when you do the full process ask at the end, "What's the next step that I need to take?" or "What do I need to know that will help me take better action with this?" The answers to these questions generally come through your sense of intuition, which makes them easier to understand, especially if you've already worked on developing this sense individually.

Natural Communication with Animals

Animals are the logical place to start in terms of exploring natural communication, as energetically their frequency is closer to ours than other parts of nature. Also, they have the added benefit of body language; once we decipher it we're able to use this as a springboard for communication.

If you're really interested in practicing natural communication with animals, I suggest that you read up on the body language of the animal you wish to practice with. Many of our human behaviors can be interpreted as acts of dominance and aggression by animals when really we're merely trying to communicate friendliness. For example, eye contact is very important for us, yet direct eye contact with animals can be very intimidating and classed as a challenge for dominance.

They also have clear warning signs that show you're making them angry. If you don't know what these are, you can miss them. In the case of cats, biting and scratching are last resorts. If this happens to you, then you've not been listening to what the cat has been communicating.

One of the biggest blocks to communicating with animals is that we humanize them. Animals have the same senses as us but they do not think, act, and sense the same way we humans do. When we make the assumption that they do, we're not able to truly hear what they're saying.

Some experts in animal communication use telepathy to communicate with animals, which is part of one of our fifty-four senses. If you're attracted to learning how to develop this skill, then the best way is by learning from someone else who is skilled in it. I'd personally recommend an awesome woman named Coryelle Kramer (www.coryellekramer.com). I've worked with her, and can confirm that not only does she know what she's talking about but the knowledge I gained from her in one session gave me the ability to communicate telepathically with animals in a way that I'd never experienced before.

Important note: Never use The Nature Process to release your emotional pain and limiting beliefs to an animal. They are not capable of recycling your energy the same way that other parts of nature are. You will harm them, as the energy you release into them will make them physically ill.

Natural Communication with Trees and Plants

Trees and plants are the easiest place for you to start in terms of practicing natural communication. They are everywhere. Unlike animals, they don't require you to invest large amounts of time and energy to ensure their well-being. However, they also have no body language, which means you need to ensure all your senses are developed to support your ability to connect. The beauty of trees is that they have the ability to blend their energetic frequency with our own, thus acting as antennae to help us tune into natural communication. Trees are both connected to the earth and reaching out towards the stars. This makes it easier for us to not only communicate with them but also to start hearing the communication of the stones, stars, and water, which I'll discuss next.

Start by getting out and going for a walk in woods. As I mentioned in chapter three, trees and plants naturally produce phytoncides, which help us reduce stress and boost our immune system. This is part of their ability to blend energetically with us.

If hugging trees is too hippy for you, simply place your hands on the trunk or sit underneath the tree with your back to it. If you're brave enough, and once you have permission of course, you can climb them. This puts you fully into their energetic frequency and connects you in a way that hugging them doesn't.

Should you be particularly interested in developing your skills in communicating with trees and plants, then you need to check out the work of Dr. Jim Conroy (www.treewhispering.com). Start by buying his book, *Tree Whispering: A nature lover's guide to touching, healing and communicating with trees, plants and all of nature.*

This will give you additional information and exercises that go beyond the purpose of this book.

Natural Communication with Stones, Stars, and Water

Stones, stars and water are the most challenging for us to connect with. Their energetic frequency, as I mentioned earlier in chapter three, is closer to the Delta brainwave state than the Theta. You have to have mastered natural presence and be adept at dropping easily into the Theta brain wave state in order to activate your ability to achieve Natural Communication with them.

If you're attracted to practicing Natural Communication with stones and water then the best way to start is by exploring them as much as possible through your fifty-four senses. Spend time playing with stones and water without any expectations of communication at first.

Physical contact with the stone or water you wish to communicate with is preferred, as this will enable you to energetically connect far easier than if there's a distance between you.

Stones, stars, and water make up the majority of the composition of the earth and the universe. Once you're able to connect with them, you're able to connect with the energy of the earth and the universe itself.

To be able to listen and truly understand what the earth and universe are communicating to you will require you to interpret the communication you receive without letting the filters of your humanity distort it. There are no human characteristics in the earth and universe at all. Their knowledge and wisdom challenge most of humanity's fundamental beliefs about how we see ourselves and the world. This type of communication is not for the faint-hearted. You need an extremely open mind.

Sadly, I've not yet met anyone who is truly skilled in this area. Much knowledge has been lost over the centuries; we are still are relying on theory and speculation as to the original purpose of Neolithic stone structures such as Stonehenge and other such standing stones. We still don't know what really exists out there among the stars.

Consolidate Natural Communication Into The Nature Process

Natural communication fits into The Nature Process in the following way:

Go out into nature and allow your natural presence to build.

Once there, connect it to your natural body.

Then find a natural attraction that resonates with you in the moment.

Consciously engage this part of nature by activating natural communication through the permission exercise. When you put it together like this, you may find that you receive information back in return. If you do, then this is a sign that you're not ready to release emotional pain and limiting beliefs to nature just yet. Instead, nature wishes to offer you guidance and insight that will help prepare you for whatever it is that you are looking to release.

When this happens, sit and notice where your senses are led. I find the use of my eyes particularly helpful here in sensing what nature want to tell me. I notice if I'm attracted to only one part of whatever I'm consciously connected to.

It's important to take your time when this happens. Allow your universal translator to work so that you get some answers. If you feel attracted to, ask more questions and explore whatever you're working on until you sense complete clarity around the information you've been given.

Then go away and think about your experience. Do any necessary research, like what I did with the cockroach I mentioned earlier. Allow yourself time to fully integrate the experience in the next few days. Whatever was communicated to you was essential in making sure that when you do The Nature Process in its entirety, like the following chapter explains, it allows you to fully release your emotional pain and limiting beliefs easily and effortlessly.

Chapter 7: Natural Release

> *There are moments when one feels free from one's own identification with human limitations and inadequacies. At such moments, one imagines that one stands on some spot of a small planet, gazing in amazement at the cold yet profoundly moving beauty of the eternal, the unfathomable: life and death flow into one, and there is neither evolution nor destiny; only being.*
>
> - Albert Einstein

I describe "being" as a state of complete balance as we stand fully in our natural power. Here you discover the truth of who you were born to be. Being is a dissolution of our mind's connection to the past and the future, allowing us to exist fully in the present: mind, body and soul. This chapter explains the last part of The Nature Process, offers some real-life examples, and shows you how to integrate your experience fully into your life.

Natural release is the final part of the process. Without engaging this, your emotional pain and limiting beliefs will remain trapped within you, blocking you from fully experiencing your natural power.

There's also a secret about your natural power that I haven't mentioned before: Just like the universe, it's infinite. The natural power you step into after going through The Nature Process for the first time is just a hint of what's to come as you release more and more emotional pain and limiting beliefs.

Within The Nature Process, this is the part of the process that takes you even deeper into a state of balance and wholeness as supported by the earth. It's where you'll start to experience and return to your natural power again and again. You'll always be able to go deeper and deeper into your natural power and discover things about yourself that you never thought possible.

You'll know that you've mastered this part of the process you find yourself naturally engaging in The Nature Process without much thought. As soon as you sense an imbalance within yourself, you'll immediately start to consciously connect to nature. Life will take on a whole new level of vividness and you'll find yourself understanding life as you've never understood it before.

Use Your Heart

The most powerful way for us to connect with the earth is with our heart. When we combine a heart connection with a physical connection through touching some part of nature with our body, we amplify the power of the earth. This is essential to The Nature Process as it allows you to go deep into a natural release.

By activating your natural presence, you make yourself more receptive to experiencing this heart/earth connection from a Theta brainwave state. The Theta brainwave state is a mental experience that allows you to drop from mind into heart and experience this connection fully.

The Institute of HeartMath in Boulder Creek, California, is pioneering research into the power of the heart. Their research shows that the heart's electromagnetic field can be detected by other people and can produce measurable effects in a person five feet away. This means that when you are fully connected to nature through your heart, you are creating an energetic bubble that encompasses not just the power of the natural attraction that is supporting you but also the power of all nature that is contained within this field.

It's through this connection that we are able to bring mind, body, and soul into a state of complete balance or coherence and release any emotional pain and limiting beliefs that are stopping us from stepping into our natural power.

Further research at the Institute of HeartMath shows that the heart possesses its own brain which is separate and distinct from our head brain. Traditionally it was thought that the head brain controlled the heart, but we now know that it's a two-way system with both head and heart communicating with each other. In fact, the electromagnetic frequency of the heart is approximately sixty times greater in amplitude than the brain.

This is what allows the earth to impact our heart's electromagnetic field and shift our emotional pain and limiting beliefs. As the earth's ability to experience growth and transformation becomes our own, the heart communicates this information to the brain creating an energetic shift that is easy and effortless.

The Power of Visualization

Back in chapter four when I talked about the natural body, I shared how the brain doesn't know the difference between real or imaginary thoughts. Brain studies show that simply thinking about an action engages the many cognitive processes within the brain involved in a real action or event.

By using visualization we can deepen the power of our natural release by focusing on how the heart connects with the earth and releases energy. This means that every time you do The Nature Process you are also training your brain to automatically do this whenever there is an imbalance within your energetic field. The more you engage with this process, the less you'll eventually have to consciously practice it!

Furthermore, being able to sense the heart's energetic frequency and feeling its connection to the earth can be challenging for some people. Visualization allows you to bypass sensing this and uses the power of the mind to ingrain The Nature Process deep within your psyche.

Once you have permission from the part of nature that is going to support you for your natural release, you visualize your heart center expanding out and connecting not just to your natural attraction but also to all of the nature within a five-foot radius.

You visualize the energy of the earth connecting with this field and then focus your attention on drawing the energy of the earth back into your heart and then out into any physical sensations you are experiencing through your natural body.

Visualize the earth's energy washing through you. If you have your hands or feet in direct contact with the earth you can visualize (and some people sense) energy coming in one hand and foot and out the other. If not, you can visualize the flow of energy from the heart in the same way it pumps blood through your body.

Either way there is a loop that brings the transformative power of the earth into whatever uncomfortable sensations your are experiencing and washes away whatever is blocking you from being in a state of balance with your mind, body, and soul, taking it back to the earth to be recycled.

The Nature Process: A Real-Time Account

As part of The Nature Process Online, I created a video in which I took myself through the entire process so that participants could have a working example of The Nature Process in action. For the purpose of this book and to help you better understand how the process works in the moment, I had the audio portion of the video transcribed. To maintain the authenticity of the experience I've kept the editing to a minimum, only making small changes that will help you fully understand the experience. Additional comments that aren't part of the recorded experience are in brackets. To do this exercise I went to the nearby forest in Ibiza and sat down near the pathway through the area.

The Transcript

Yes, you will notice that I am stroking a cat as I'm speaking to you. I had the wonderful honor and privilege to have two of my landlady's cats, Biscuit and Hindu, follow me all the way from the house, all the way out here to actually do this process down the country road for about five minutes. [My relationship with them was developed through the use of natural communication so this shows the power of that by itself].

Truly touching moment, I feel very privileged that I have that much of a connection with them that they will do that for me. They are obviously here for whatever reason—to support or just give whatever.

I leave Ibiza in less than a week, and although I know I'll be coming back, I'm going to be packing up my room. I've got about three or four months of travel coming up—book writing and other stuff.

What has been really interesting for me is I noticed that I'm not excited about it. In actual fact, I almost feel slightly overwhelmed. What is really fascinating is that normally I love to go traveling. Yet here I have the same sense of loss as if I'm packing up, leaving, moving on, and not coming back.

It's the last six months that I've been here and integrating where I'm living. There are now five cats, three dogs, a beautiful garden, and a wonderful sense of community. Somebody new has just moved in who's got a seven-year-old kid. This is actually everything I've ever wanted in a place to stay.

I feel the sadness, and what is interesting is that as I reflect on this with you I realize that there is still some sadness around the fact that I still have stuff left at my ex-boyfriend's house in Galicia, Spain, from about three years ago. It's still packed up in boxes that I haven't been back to collect. When I was there I really thought I'd found my permanent home there. It was really difficult when I left. I didn't even know if I was coming back to Spain.

There is some energy being triggered by what I'm going through now that's connected to there as well. When you're doing the nature process, you don't need to be in depth, but this is the first thing that you need to know: "What is it that I want to shift there?" This is what I'm looking at.

Then you come out into nature. As I look and focus on my natural presence, I've chosen a spot to sit down that is interesting to me. I was attracted to this spot. It felt right to sit down on a lovely rock just at the side of a little path. This little path is just off the country road, and as you can see behind me, there are just lots of these awesome bushes. I have no idea what they are. I've got the same in front of me.

To the left there's a grove of pine trees with pine cones in them. There's a nice stillness in the air. I just saw a little bird moving the branches, fluttering about from branch to branch. I hear more birds singing. There's all this greenery around me. There's even a dead tree further down in the distance. I like it because it's so straight and then it stretches up.

Then I can see hills in the distance. I've got Biscuit, who is a ginger tom, lying on the ground next to me enjoying the nature too. Hindu has disappeared into the bushes. She's very timid.

There are some dry brown flowery things on the bush—dying flowers, because of the heat. As I look around, all of this green and brown contrasts against the sky. A little Sycamore leaf swirls down, and down, and down onto the ground. That was pretty cool.

Again, noticing the birds' movements in the trees. The color of the sky is a lovely pale blue and I notice just how the light is reflecting on it because there are these clouds. Where the light is hitting the clouds there are candy floss clouds. These are the clouds that when I was like seven years old, I believed care bears lived on. The contrast is just incredible, and then when the clouds are not illuminated by the light, they go this darker gray wispiness.

As I'm sitting here, my bum is quite sore on this rock. I've got dirt in my hands from stroking the ground. The cat comes back over.

This is really about becoming fully aware of the natural environment and giving yourself time to feel this connection. The cat is licking my fingers with his raspy tongue. This is what natural presence is about.

Now, this might take five minutes, it might take twenty minutes. If you're really, really, stressed or upset, becoming so fully aware of nature and fully present within it will take longer. It's taken me up to an hour before if I've been really annoyed with lots of stuff going on in my head.

I feel so awesome sitting out here. It's so beautiful. I hope the camera is picking up all the birds' songs that are going on behind me. The fact that I have this ginger tom as a part of it—by the way, I always wanted a ginger tom, who has just bit my finger—is really awesome.

[This point in the video is about seven minutes in and throughout all this part of the video the ginger cat has been rubbing himself around me and I've been stroking him while talking.]

I feel my natural presence, along with the cat, who's still here and hasn't moved off, which is good, because I'm now going to move into talking about natural body. When I actually think about moving I'm noticing that I feel like I'm swelling. There's a slight nauseous sensation and it feels like something is stuck in my throat.

There's a lot of tightness and heaviness in my chest. I want to cough. I can feel a tightness in my throat. I have all these sensations going on here, even a slight headache when I actually think about this upcoming moving, traveling, how it's tied to Galicia.

Even as I focus on my natural body I'm still maintaining my natural presence. I'm still focusing and looking around. The contrasting colors of green in the leaves with a dark green that I can sense in the distance.

This is where I'm moving into natural attractions. I'm present to nature. I'm conscious of this tightness tickly yucky feeling that it's kind of running up and down my chest area.

I'm looking around and thinking, "What am I attracted to?" I was really attracted to the green but not enough to actually want to work with that.

As I'm sitting here, I'm becoming even more conscious of the fact that there is this wonderful big rock with some moss on it. I like the feeling of my feet underneath it, so I am really attracted to this rock. I love running my fingers over it and feeling how it feels.

I really like this rock because it is strong and it is stable. Strong, stable, it's powerful and it's just here. It's also connected to everywhere else in the world.

This acknowledgment that I am attracted to working with this rock and releasing the emotional pain and limiting beliefs that come up around my imminent move brings pricks of tears to my eyes. The cat just came over and bit me again.

[While animals may be present to support us through The Nature Process, remember that you can never use them for this process. Not even if you get consent from them. Releasing our emotional pain and limiting beliefs directly into animals leaves them with it. To consciously do this is abuse.]

I'm just realizing that I am really strong, powerful, steady, present and connected everywhere all over the world. Even though I am going, there will still be a part of me here in Ibiza.

There's a lovely little fly that has just appeared at this moment. Flies have a special significance connected to my brother for me. I'm going to take that as a sign that my brother in spirit is here supporting me. I'm experiencing more tear pricks in my eyes, which is again a sign of energy shifting within the natural body.

Having found my natural attraction to this rock, I literally cannot stop touching it. I'm going to take a moment and ask for permission. I will talk my way through this as well and explain to you exactly what I'm doing. For me, I do not often do formalized, "Can I have permission to connect with you?" statements.

I'm laughing now because when I just said that I got the sensation of a response that was translated as, "Why, yes you can!" I guess I've got my permission! I'm still laughing and this makes me feel so good that it's one of the ways I'm interpreting consent.

I'm sitting here, smiling and laughing after having little tear pricks from the heaviness of the sensations in my natural body. This is a sign of a connection shift and that I have permission from this rock to integrate with it. My hands are physically connected to the rock and I'm very aware of the power of the rock underneath me.

Now I'm going to take a moment to drop into my heart center, which is ever more important considering this is where I'm sensing all this stuff within me. As I do I feel a little bit nauseous and like I want to burp.

For those of you who don't know me very well, burping is one of the ways that I manage to shift energy without being sick. You don't have to do this. I did have a friend who said to me when I told her about creating this video, "What? Are you going to let people see you burp?" Apparently so.

As I connect to my heart center I can feel the connection to the rock. From my heart center I'm aware of how the energetic field emanates out. I'm going to sit here and close my eyes for this because this is what feels right for me. I am going to feel the strength and power of the rock at the same time I feel that heavy sensation of my emotional pain and limiting belief.

Through visualization and sensing I'm aware of my energy field and that through the connection of both my hands and legs with the rock that they're drawing up energy and deepening my connection to the rock.

The cat just came up, brushed against me, and bit me again. I'm starting to focus on connecting the energy of the rock with the sensations in my natural body. Now I'm yawning. Yes, more yawning and a little fart. Stuff is shifting. I can feel a rumbling sensation in my stomach.

The tightness in my chest is actually increasing as I'm doing this. What's good is that I'm actually getting a tighter pain behind my head. Sometimes the intensity of a sensation in the body increases before shifting.

I'm conscious of Hindu meowing now. I've got her too so now I have the support of two cats, as you can see from the animals coming up around me.

Cats are my power animals. I have a special affinity with them. The fact that I have these two cats who followed me out the house and are here to help me release this is really humbling for me. Really humbling to know that I have managed to get that level of trust with them.

They've come along and they're helping trigger a release because I'm feeling very emotional. I'm focusing on breathing through this, but as I'm breathing through this I've got the tears going there. And more burping.

I'm not really a big crier now. I spent a lot of time crying after my brother died, and even with my health problems, if I needed to cry, I'd cry. Now I prefer shifting energy through burping, through breathing, through yawning, through moving my body, and as we're talking I can feel my shoulders moving.

As I sit here in my little energetic bubble with the support of the rocks and knowing that these two cats are here to help me tap into my wisdom I can even feel my nose running. Great—more shifting, there's stuff happening there.

I see people walking along the path. I am going to ignore them and keep on going even as the cat meows. The tightness in my chest is not as tight as it was before but I still have band of tightness around my head.

Even though I've opened my eyes and acknowledged a "Hello" there to the two women who walked past, I'm now sitting here again with my eyes shut.

This is what I love about the process. The fact that they have no freaking idea what I'm doing. I recognize them as two ladies that I've spoken to before. They know that I make videos, which is cool.

As all this is going on remember you have to go into this with no expectations. The fact that I have been able to continue and acknowledge the people coming through is huge for me. So is going through this process with you.

This is powerful. You will see I talk a lot. But as I'm talking to you, what is interesting is literally I am sitting here and all of that tightness within my chest...large burp. Pardon me.

That's another shift there. I'm releasing all that tightness in my chest, and it's quite soft. It's gentle.

I'm going to be blowing my nose very, very well after this!

This is a simple way to release emotional pain and limiting beliefs because you're focusing on the sensations. I'm still conscious of that sensation of tightness in my head. There is pressure and I can acknowledge that this pressure has actually been there for the last few days. It's kind of like been building up. This has been building up without me even noticing it.

Burping again. Oh goodness.

Even as I'm talking I'm releasing. I can feel my stomach jiggling but as I shift...huge burp. That might have been gross but that was a really powerful energetic shift.

If was so powerful that the sun shined brighter as if to acknowledge that. With that burp, there's a sense of lightness...more burping...Obviously a lot more to shift than I've thought.

Now the ginger cat has disappeared and the black cat has come out, which I will reflect on this afterwards as to why the ginger tom was supporting me and now the black shy timid cat is coming out at this stage.

More burping.

Burping and yawning are the preferred ways of my body. I had a little bit of tears but I'm not a crier. Some of you might be criers and if I need to cry, I would cry.

I can feel that the pain in my head is deadening slightly. I feel a lot more open in my head but I notice there's a wheeze or two coming up as I breathe. Lungs are associated with sadness and grief. I've been doing work with my lungs recently. If I breathe through my nose I don't notice the wheeze as much as I do when I breathe through my mouth.

More burping.

Now both cats are out next to me. I get a sense that I am finished. I have no idea what I was releasing. I only know what it was in relation to. I don't need to know.

When you release emotional pain and limiting beliefs, you can gain insight into the next step, but only the next step, because nature only exists in the present moment. Burp. I'm not finished shifting this. Thank goodness. What I love about this process is that I can just sit here and burp. Nobody would know what I'm really doing here. If they noticed my burping they'd just think I'm really uncouth. This is the beauty of the Nature Process.

There is little more tightness coming up. I thought I was finished but I'm not. Burp.

[I would have preferred to have been done. Nevertheless I hope that from reading about this experience as it happened, you've got the general gist of this.]

I have these cats next to me and they're so freaking cute. This is what I get to come back to. It's not going anywhere.

I don't need to be sad to leave. I am here, and just like the rock I'm a part of nature. I'm everywhere. I will tap into that, bring it back, and forget the silly idea that I'm leaving anything.

This is my home. The whole world is my home. I'm just going to go visit another aspect of it. I'm going to see my Scottish family instead of being with my Spanish family, write a book and travel to France and the USA. There's a lot of really awesome exciting things coming up which I've forgotten about because of that heaviness I felt before.

I've finished shifting now because I feel good. All of that tightness, that heaviness and pressure is gone. Even the wheeze that was present just before is not the same wheeze. My lungs have shifted stuff in there too, which is awesome.

That has made me feel really happy and really excited. The next step that I know that I'm going to do which is completely actually logical is I'm going to go and pack my suitcase and pack up some of my room to reflect this transition. I'm going to pack up so then I can shift into "Traveler Tabi," who only has her backpack with all her electrical equipment and very few clothes.

Just the thought of that is so exciting. I have my release and I feel super freaking happy. I'm going to go and pack my stuff, transfer myself into "Traveler Tabi" so that I'm already traveling. I'm already on an adventure and I'm already home. Now I can't wait.

I just want to smile. I want to go dance. I feel so much better than I have all day.

[The video finishes at 28 minutes.]

I hope than reading through my experience has been useful for you and that it helps you to go through The Nature Process so that you too can get rid of your emotional pain and limiting beliefs and come back to a place of excitement and balance in which you too step into your natural power.

A Different Perspective on The Nature Process

The more examples you have of The Nature Process in action, the easier it is for you to get an idea of how it works and what you should be doing when you're out in nature by yourself. One of The Nature Process Online participants, who I personally guided through the process, wrote a blog post about her experience. Sara Sanderson (www.sarajsanderson.com) gave me permission to share an excerpt of it here with you to offer you a different perspective on going through The Nature Process. You can also see where I guided and supported her to get a further idea of how you can guide and support yourself with the help of this book.

Sara's Blog Post

The day of the session I felt called to go to a local cemetery where I'd been for the first time in years just the day before with a friend. It turned out to be an ideal place for what unfolded.

With Tabitha asking the questions, I first became present in nature by describing my surroundings and then noticed what I was naturally attracted to. I sat barefoot on the grass, an area of the cemetery I was guided to by a squirrel, who then ran up a tree and sat there the whole time. It was like he was watching over me during the session. Every now and then I could hear him moving around high up in the branches.

I sat feeling safe and comfortable as I held on to a short stem of a plant explaining to Tabitha what I wanted to explore during the session. However, when I asked for permission to connect with it to support me during the session, the answer was no; and it was an adjoining leaf, soft and smooth to the touch, where I found permission to continue.

The texture of the leaf was gorgeous to touch, delicate yet strongly rooted to the ground and firmly connected to the earth. With the support of nature I explored what was at the core of my perceived block to receiving my birthright of abundance in monetary terms. Delving into my unconscious mind, I sensed there was an invisible force-field that protected me, and although I had room to move around within this bubble with its transparent force-field wall, I felt it was preventing certain things from getting in (such as my fullness to health, money and intimacy).

I used the support of the leaf rooted in the earth to start altering the force-field. In my mind's eye I visualized the force-field pulsing, and then it started to vibrate rapidly. As the intensity grew so did fear rise up inside me, so I stopped before any damage to the force-field occurred. It just didn't feel safe to break it.

The reasons why included "I would die if it came down" and "I wouldn't be strong enough without it." Clearly these are not logical responses but our unconscious mind, and how it affects the nervous system is real to the body and has an impact on our external circumstances and situations.

Tabitha asked whether there was another part of nature I was attracted to that might help support me further. As I looked around, a butterfly flew past and my eyes followed it and then my body moved too. I relocated to another patch of grass where I felt drawn to what I descried to Tabitha as a warrior leaf.

Tabitha was quick to explain that the warrior was of course me (the whole nature process is a reflection of self). As I held on to the warrior leaf I could easily embody my inner warrior, and together we shook and vibrated the force-field until it shattered into a billion pieces.

I no longer felt fear, in fact I felt expansive and powerful wanting to scream out loud "Freedom!" I was reminded by the lines sang by Caliban in Shakespeare's *The Tempest*, and for me it was a clear reminder to my mind that it's not the master of who I am:

"Ban, 'ban, Ca-caliban Sara

Has a new master. So get a new servant.

Freedom, what a wonderful day, wonderful day, freedom, freedom, wonderful day, freedom!"

Tabitha supported me to anchor this feeling of freedom, and being in and supported by nature so I could draw upon it whenever I choose.

I noticed a single ant on my hand and a single worm circling around the base of the warrior leaf. It didn't occur to me at the time how unusual it was to have seen only one squirrel, a single butterfly, a single ant, and a single worm. As I call upon symbolic meaning in the coaching I do (the unconscious uses symbols and metaphors to communicate), I decided to look up what each creature meant, and was delighted by what I read as each one supported my nature process experience perfectly.

I feel a shift certainly happened and transformation is taking place regarding abundance flowing and being received. There may well be more work to do in keeping down the perceived need for a force-field around me. I will continue to explore with the support of nature as I progress my business and continue to create and manifest my heart's desires.

How to Fully Integrate Your Experience into Your Psyche

It takes a couple of days for your experience with The Nature Process to fully integrate within you. The reason being is that what you experience while in a Theta brainwave state says in the Theta brainwave state. As you move out of this state into either an Alpha state, which is a relaxed but alert state, or the Beta state, you are unable to access the information you've received.

It's the same process involved with dreams. As you wake up and get caught up in the busy-ness of your daily life you tend to forget what you dreamt about. Sometimes fragments of the dream will work their way into your consciousness and you get a flash of recall.

As with the permission exercise in the previous chapter, these questions are adapted from Dr. Mike's book *Reconnecting with Nature: Finding Wellness through Restoring Your Bond with the Earth*. They're what I asked my private clients to complete and send back to me as I taught them during our sessions together what you now know as The Nature Process. They're also similar to part of the coursework I did in my Masters in Applied Ecopsychology.

I recommend doing them immediately after you've gone through The Nature Process, as the experience is more vivid in your memory. Then after a couple of days go back and read over what you've written and see if you have any additional insights that have taken your universal translator a while to interpret.

1. How did you do the exercise, and what happened when you did it?
2. On a scale of 1-10 (1 = very poor 5 = average 10 = extremely great) how good did you feel before starting as per the instructions?
3. On a scale of 1-10 (1 = very poor 5 = average 10 = extremely great) how good did you feel after doing this exercise?
4. What were the three most important things you learned whilst doing the exercise?
5. Finish this sentence in three different ways (e.g. I feel the wind in my hair and I know I'm healing): I am a person who gets good feelings when ___.
6. Does this exercise enhance your sense of self-worth? Your trustfulness of nature?
7. How would you feel if this experience was taken away from you?
8. Did you have any negative signals (feelings, memories) during the exercise?
9. Do you have any fears, concerns, or reservations about moving forward?
10. What one or two keywords symbolise this experience for you?
11. What short power sentence coveys the contribution this exercise makes to your growth?
12. Who could you share this experience with?

If you're not attracted to journaling about your experience you can also use audio and video to capture the present moment. The challenge with using technology is that it too emits electromagnetic frequencies. If you aren't fully grounded into a Theta brainwave state then you can actually knock yourself out of it and weaken the power of The Nature Process. If you are going to do this make sure that you create some distance between you and whatever equipment you choose to use.

You may also want to ground your experience into a physical movement, which I did with Sara though she doesn't mention it in her sharing of her experience. Once you have the sensation of feeling good and complete around your experience focus on the feeling. Ask yourself what movement would best represent the way you feel in the moment. Some people have done hand waves, a shoulder shrug. a hand gesture or just even a small movement with part of their body. Once you have your movement repeat it a few times. This connects the movement to the way you feel. Then at any time you can make this movement and remind yourself of your experience and the way you felt at the time. It's no substitute for being out in nature though it's a great tool to use whenever you can't get outside for whatever reason.

Some Final Reminders

Providing you follow the guidelines within this book, there is no right or wrong way to do The Nature Process. As you engage with nature you'll find that you have your own way of working with it that is unique to you.

The biggest thing you need to do is trust. Trust that your natural body knows exactly how to naturally release your emotional pain and limiting beliefs without any effort from your mind. Trust that you already know how to do this. You've just forgotten. All this book is doing is making you conscious of knowledge that lies within your subconscious.

All the background and information provided in this book is to allow your mind to accept that this not only is possible but that it's simple to do. The Nature Process is not complicated.

1. Set the intention for what emotional pain and limiting belief that you want to use nature to shift.
2. Go outside and experience nature through your natural presence.
3. Become aware of what sensations arise in your natural body when you think about what you want to release.
4. Focus on a part of nature through your natural attractions.
5. Use your natural communication to get permission to connect with that part of nature.
6. Visualize your natural release and let the power of nature move you back into a state of balance and wholeness with your own natural power.

You do not have to force anything. It will happen automatically with or without you visualizing it. If you start to feel frustrated, then find another natural attraction to support you to go deeper just like I guided Sara to do.

Remember to thank nature for supporting you afterwards as you would any other helping professional. After all, you're getting nature's support for free any time you want.

Last but not least, remain in a state of openness and suspend judgment before, during and after The Nature Process. Don't create expectations of how you think the process should and will work for you. Let go of whatever is blocking you from being in your natural power.

Become the person you are born to be.

It really is this simple.

Chapter 8: Get Out of Your Own Way

The true value of a human being is determined primarily by the measure and the sense in which he has attained to liberation from the self.

- Albert Einstein

If anything is going to stop you from successfully using The Nature Process, it's going to be yourself. We are our own worst enemies. At times when we know that something has the potential to change our life, we create resistance.

The cause is fear of the unknown. As you know by now, fear is nothing more than a sign that you need to reconnect with nature! But sometimes it's not that easy. We have become so used to who we are with our emotional pain and limiting beliefs that we can't imagine ourselves without them.

It's like picking up a heavy stone and carrying it around with us for ages. After a while you stop noticing the stone and start adapting to it. You become so used to the stone that you can't imagine letting go of it. In fact you're actually quite comfortable carrying it.

Carrying a stone is a great exercise for you to do out in nature to allow you to experience what it feels like to feel resistance to growth and transformation within your life. It shows you that once you let the stone go you actually feel so much lighter and better than you did before.

Yet sometimes it's not that easy. This chapter focuses specifically on the challenges that may come up for you as you work through The Nature Process, and offers additional information and practical tips to help you work through this. It will make it easy for you to let go of what's holding you back so you can fully release all your emotional pain and limiting beliefs and step into your natural power.

Don't Let Yourself Get Distracted

In our modern, busy world there are so many distractions, and it's easy to get caught up in them. I eat, breath and sleep nature, literally as well as metaphorically. Yet even I still find myself getting distracted and putting off going outside to experience any part of The Nature Process. I might drink a little bit too much wine or spend time surfing the internet wondering what on earth I was looking for again. That's the moment I put everything down and go to nature.

If you don't know why you're doing something, then it's a good chance that you're engaging in distraction behavior. This is a maladaptive coping mechanism that helps numb our senses of pain, distress, and fear without actually allowing ourselves to reconnect to other senses and truly feel better.

Now it's important to state that there's actually nothing wrong with distraction behaviors. As long as you recognize them for what they truly are. Sometimes we're not ready to face our emotional pain and limiting beliefs and let them go. That's ok. The most important thing here is that you don't judge yourself and say you should be doing something different. That'll just add to the emotional pain and limiting beliefs you have to shift.

The problem is distracting yourself without actually acknowledging that it's a distraction behavior. That's when you'll start making all sorts of justifications to yourself as to why you're not going outside and doing any of The Nature Process. If you're truly not interested in going outside, you'll be able to acknowledge that you're just not attracted to it. However, if you're not going outside because it's too cold, or raining, or too hot, or you've got more important things to do, then that's distraction. Don't buy into it.

Own Your Emotions

Another way of getting in our own way when we start to practice The Nature Process is by pretending that we what feel isn't really coming from us. We humans are very good at putting our emotions onto someone else and empathizing with what they're going through. The problem here is that most people I've come across who say they're "empaths" are in actual fact sensing their own emotions rather than those of the other person.

The best examples I have of this are the people who have empathized with me in the past over my brother's death. When it comes to an anniversary or special occasion, they've said they can understand how I'm feeling and offer me their condolences. What they're really sensing is their own baggage getting in the way.

I don't regret the death of my brother. It's the inspiration behind everything I do. I've worked hard to ensure that the anniversary of my brother's death is a celebration of his life and of growth and transformation. That's the main reason The Nature Process Online launches every May. It's a way of honoring my brother and giving him a lasting legacy in this world that reflects the true essence of who he is. This excites me. I look forward to May and to what I can do every year to make the celebration of his life bigger and better. You have no idea what I'm feeling unless you can sense the lightness and love surrounding this.

This ability to transfer our emotions onto someone else works with nature, too. There are many people who talk about how they can sense the pain and distress of the earth due to the damage we humans are doing to it. They are sensing their own emotions about what humans are doing to the earth, not the earth's.

I've mentioned this before but it's necessary to repeat it as it's so important. You'll know that you're not owning your own emotions if you get defensive and feel the need to let other people know how you feel, often interrupting them as you do. This is the driving factor behind so much of the environmental activism movement. The whole "look at what you're doing to the planet" and the guilt and shame they try to make us feel is really about their unwillingness to accept that these are their own emotions.

Instead they try to make themselves feel better by consoling themselves that they at least are doing something. This way they never have to own their own guilt and shame over their individual behavior and our collective behavior towards the earth in the past. When you don't own your emotions, you have no hope of changing them.

Once you own how you feel, then you can let it go. That's why The Nature Process is so powerful. It allows you to do this both for your emotional pain and limiting beliefs towards things that have happened in the past and for any guilt and shame you may experience over how you've treated nature in the past.

True environmental activism comes from a place of hope and inspiration. It encourages us to take action by saying look at what we could achieve both for ourselves and nature.

Explore Your Beliefs About Nature

We all have hidden beliefs about nature. Many of them aren't even our own. They've been culturally ingrained into us over the last two thousand plus years.

The first chapter of the Bible (Genesis 1:28) says:

"And God blessed them, and God said unto them, Be fruitful, and multiply, and replenish the earth, and subdue it: and have dominion over the fish of the sea, and over the fowl of the air, and over every living thing that moveth upon the earth."

This belief has driven our modern western Christian society forward, giving us God's permission to basically do what we want to the earth. What's tragic about this belief is that it was deliberately created to discredit the pagan religions that came before. The Druids worshipped outside in sacred groves of trees. Many pagan Greek and Roman gods had their sacred sites outside in nature too. I'm don't think whoever wrote the Bible fully understood the implications of what they were doing.

This belief has been reinforced again and again throughout history. In the sixteenth century, Sir Francis Bacon argued that the only way to gain objective scientific knowledge was to separate ourselves from nature and to "conquer and subdue" it. Incidentally, he also referred to nature as a "common harlot," thus helping to create the idea that nature and women were linked.

Bacon developed his ideas right in the middle of the witch trials that spread across Europe between the fifteenth and the eighteenth centuries. This was a period of time when thousands of victims—primarily women—were accused of witchcraft and burned at the stake. Many of them were natural healers, women who lived alone with cats, or women who couldn't keep their mouths shut. Just as well we've moved on from that time period. I wouldn't have lasted long!

Rene Descartes, the man responsible for creating mind/body dualism as mentioned in chapter one, claimed that the goal of mind/body dualism was to "make ourselves masters and possessors of nature."

John Locke, the English philosopher and physician who was one of the most influential thinkers of the Enlightenment, told us that, "Land that is left wholly to nature, is called as indeed it is waste."

Whether you like it or not, these beliefs have been floating around influencing you since you were a child. They drive our behavior in many areas, not just in relationship to nature. In the fact that we've been taught to hate our bodies you can see the influence of Rene Descartes.

Whenever you feel blocked during any part of exploration of The Nature Process, it's worth checking to see if you have any beliefs that may be getting in the way of your experience. Once you uncover a belief that contradicts what I'm teaching in this book, you can take it to nature to experience the truth for yourself. In this way you can heal an unconscious wound that's partly responsible for keeping you disconnected not just from nature but from your own Natural Power.

Don't Buy Into "Green" Marketing

With the rise of awareness of global warming and climate change has also come the rise of "green" business. There's a lot of money to be made from our fear about what's happening to the planet and the chemicals that we're pumping into the environment. This is leading to a lot of products coming into the marketplace that aren't really beneficial to us or the planet, and may actually keep us in a state of disconnect.

Green cleaning products have been developed that remove toxic chemicals and replace them with more environmentally friendly one. These cleaning products tend to be more expensive than average products, but they make you feel good as you use them. You're doing something for yourself and the planet.

Yet many of these "natural" products are not even natural. In June 2014 Ecover, one of the leading pioneers of green cleaning products, admitted that they were using ingredients derived from "synthetically modified organisms" which are the next wave of GMOs to enter our marketplace. Synthetic biology has been classed as "extreme genetic engineering." Yeah, because that's natural!

The thing that pisses me off the most about this is that all you need to successfully clean your house is bicarbonate of soda and vinegar. You can buy these cheaply at any supermarket, do a little bit of research online on how to use them for different things and you have the most natural cleaning products ever. They are the cheapest too.

Another area where "green" marketing is prevalent is the beauty industry. There are all these wonderful products marketing as natural and soft and gentle on your skin. Yet when you actually look at the ingredients they're still using chemicals that have been connected to causing cancer. The easiest rule with beauty products is that if you wouldn't eat whatever it is, then don't put it on your body.

As someone who has been so sensitive to issues like this from birth, I'm personally invested in this. I know how painful it is to experience ill health because the products we're using are toxic to us and actually create more problems than they solve.

Over the years as I've searched to find creams that were helpful for my eczema, I've had to tolerate itchy inflamed skin made worse by the very treatments that claimed to help them, some of them prescribed by the medical establishment itself.

As a last resort I started looking at natural ingredients and how they could help me. That's what's made the biggest difference to my health. Now I look for a natural herbal option before anything else. In the process of doing so, I save so much money it's ridiculous.

Even our food has been taken over by "green" marketing. If you go to any health food shop you'll see a bewildering array of foods that you've never heard of, all packaged up as the next super food designed to bring your body back into balance and counter act the effects of the toxic environment we now live in. Not only have they come from goodness knows where in the world, but they also quite conveniently cost a lot of money.

We're also told by some people that the best diet for us is an organic, plant-based diet, and if we don't follow this we're going straight to hell. Now I'm not making light of the fact that the conditions in which we farm animals are horrific. The practices involved in the production of our food, especially the meat industry, are some of the most distressing things I've ever witnessed.

I'm making light of the fact that so many people want to tell us what to eat and make it so complicated when nature makes it so simple for us. Whether it's plant based or not, eat what nature provides for you in the local area that you live in, when it's in season, and you won't go wrong. If you grow it yourself then it's even better or, which is my personal favorite, get someone else to grow it for you.

Michael Pollen, author of *In Defense of Food: An Eater's Manifesto*, sums up the only diet advice you'll ever need: "Eat food. Not too much. Mostly plants." The only problem with this is where's the money in that?

All of this might seem as if I've digressed slightly from taking about The Nature Process. I've not. If you buy into the "green" marketing, you buy into a disconnect from nature that will not allow you to experience the full power of The Nature Process, and furthermore may cause you to discount your experiences because they run contradictory to what you hear in the media.

Observe Your Language

When it comes to nature, there's empowered language and there's disempowered language. I mentioned earlier in the chapter about how much of the environmental activist movement is tied into trying to guilt and shame us into making changes. This is further supported by the language that's used by many in the environmental movement. We talk about saving the planet and protecting it. We say that it's a fragile planet and is at peril.

This language actually blocks you from being able to consciously connect to nature. If this is your perception of the nature then how can you have enough trust in that you believe it'll be able to help you fully shift your emotional pain and limiting beliefs?

One of the reasons that I grounded natural communication in chapter six into James Lovelock's Gaia hypothesis is to help you see just how adept the planet is at keeping itself in balance and has been able to do so for billions of years. The planet knows more about what it's doing that we do. To pretend any different is to commit the cardinal sin of being human: that of assuming we know best.

If we humans were truly bringing the planet completely out of balance, nature would have wiped us out by now. If we continue our destructive behavior, then that's probably what's going to happen. The planet is not going to get caught up in guilt and shame over whether or not we survive. Those emotions belong firmly in the realm of humans.

It's our own fear over the thought of being wiped out that drives so much of our actions towards the environment. Remember, fear is a sign that we are disconnected from nature and that we need to reconnect. Any action we take towards saving or protecting the environment from this place is actually going to have the opposite effect.

The beautiful thing about James Lovelock is that when he initially developed the Gaia hypothesis he was one of the alarmists who predicted that the earth would be destroyed by human activity by now. Yet his perspective has changed dramatically. In a UK TV interview in April 2014 he turned round and actually heavily criticized the United Nations Intergovernmental Panel on Climate Change (IPCC) as relying on guesses as to what is really happening on earth right now.

Scientists claim that we are in the age of the sixth great extinction, brought on by human behavior. This is when there's a widespread and rapid decrease of the amount of life on earth. The last time this happened was 65 million years ago with the extinction of the dinosaurs. Their death made room for mammals to become the dominant class on earth and for us to exist as we now do today.

We've got it wrong. It's not extinction. It's evolution. The only question we need to be asking ourselves is whether we are going to evolve along with the earth or be wiped out like the dinosaurs.

When you ensure that your language supports the fact that the earth is a self-regulating complex organism that has been capable of sustaining life for 4.5 billion years, you are able to consciously connect to that power and recognize that it is a reflection of your own natural power.

Pay attention to the language you use when talking or thinking about nature. That will shape how far you go with The Nature Process.

Nature Reflects You

What nature offers us when we consciously connect with it is a mirror in which we are able to see ourselves. It is a way for us to see the strength and power that lies within us.

In order for us to see this we must use our fifty-four senses to follow our natural attractions. Any pain, distress or fear that we experience in nature is a reflection back to us that we are not connected. We are not connected to nature and we are not connected to ourselves.

If you follow The Nature Process as I've outlined here in the book, you will not experience pain, distress, and fear in nature. If you do then it's imperative that you shift and connect to something that makes you feel good.

This is something you will have to practice. We are not trained by our society to naturally move towards things that make us feel good. We're trained to make the most of a bad situation. That's why so many of us who have bought into what society tells us we should do with our lives achieve the goals society has set up but then still feel unfulfilled and unsatisfied with our lives.

Furthermore, if you are focusing on the pain and destruction of nature then you are focusing on your own pain and destruction. We don't heal by staying connected to what's broken. We heal by finding new natural attractions that make us feel good and will support us as we grow and transform.

Always look for what makes you feel good in nature. As you do you'll start to look for what makes you feel good in all aspects of your life. This is how you step fully into your natural power easily and effortlessly.

Let Your Imagination Run Free

Dr. Mike of Project NatureConnect, who developed the work around the fifty-four senses, natural attractions, and the permission exercise that form that basis for the process in this book, has a great expression: "I'll trust science when it figures out how to turn grass into milk."

Don't put all your trust into science. While it's great for helping us understand the world that we live in better, it doesn't know everything. There are just as many blinkered by their beliefs scientists as there are blinkered by their beliefs new-agers.

Furthermore, science can have a habit of making your forget just how mysterious and magical nature is. As Einstein said:

"There are two ways to live your life. Once as though nothing is a miracle. The other as though everything is a miracle."

If you are not viewing your life as a miracle while you go through The Nature Process, then it's a sign you're not fully engaging with it. I promise you, what's contained in this book will take you on a journey into nature that you've never experienced before.

It's possible that as you go further into The Nature Process you start discounting your natural attractions. You start to limit what you think is possible and you don't allow yourself to fully explore where you can go with nature.

The thing is, you can go as deep into nature as you allow yourself to. In the introduction I offered you the opportunity to take the red pill, enter the rabbit hole, and see how far it'll take you into the earth. Think of Alice's disbelief as she entered Wonderland and how curious she found it. As you consciously connect with nature you'll experience the same thing.

When you engage in natural communication with nature, you get insights that may seem a little bizarre. These insights will test your understanding of both yourself and the world. They're supposed to.

Take a moment and think about it. I have conversations with bugs, as I've told you about in this book! Do you know how bizarre that is for me? As I worked on this chapter I had a flying beetle land on my keyboard and crawl around it while a moth has danced around my head before landing on my leg. It's taken a huge stretch of my imagination to accept that there was conversation going on between us. In fact while I have an idea of what they were communicating, I still need some time to fully process that.

It's just like the whole Roachie story. I mean, seriously. I carried a cockroach in my luggage to release it back into the wild when I arrived in France! Who on earth does that?

You have no idea what's possible when you fully connect to nature in a conscious manner. This book is only the beginning. I've focused on consciously connecting to nature for nearly thirteen years and have a deeper understanding of it than most people I meet. Yet I know I'm just at the tip of the iceberg in what's possible for me to learn from nature both about myself and the world as I keep doing The Nature Process.

I trust nature. I let go and let my imagination run free as I engage in The Nature Process because I know that it's only through this that I can keep on stepping up into my natural power.

Whatever you get when you consciously connect with nature through The Nature Process is right even if you initially interpret it wrong. Trust it. Go with it. Keep at this. Develop your imagination so that it's so powerful you never doubt the information you receive. Even if it takes you a while to properly translate it!

Start Asking "What If?"

Instead of thinking that you're crazy when you start going through The Nature Process, ask, "What if?"

Instead of thinking that you're making up what you're getting from nature as you consciously connect to it, ask, "What if?"

When you let go of your emotional pain and limiting belief in nature and you find it so easy and effortless that you start to doubt that it's actually happened, ask, "What if?"

If you experienced something during any part of The Nature Process that really challenged you in such a way that you started to doubt what happened, ask, "What if?"

This is the key to suspending disbelief. It keeps the door open for you to integrate any experience you have over the next few days. Sleeping on an experience has a wonderful way for helping you to truly understand what's happened as you let go of your emotional pain and limiting beliefs.

Leave room for the growth and transformation that you gain from going through The Nature Process fully to bloom and blossom into something beyond anything you've ever know before.

Like the L'Oreal adverts state, "You're worth it!"

Stay Connected

Our natural state of being with nature is a state of connection. To be in a state of disconnect from nature is a learned experience. If you find yourself getting frustrated with any part of The Nature Process, ask yourself what you are doing in that moment to keep yourself in a state of disconnect.

Many times when this happens you'll find that you are not fully engaging your natural presence, so your Theta brain wave state is not stable. You're then letting your mind get in the way and judge what you're experiencing or interpret it incorrectly due to some of the things I've mentioned earlier. Remember there is no right or wrong in nature, there is only nature.

If you're not able to stay connected to nature even when your mind questions it, you've not gone deep enough into your natural presence. Ideally you need to use your natural presence every day, even if it's just for five minutes as you stare out the kitchen window while preparing dinner.

You'll find that it actually requires more effort to stay disconnected that it does to remain connected. Many times when people feel disconnected from nature it's because they've chosen to focus on the three senses (pain, distress, fear) that are signals for us to reconnect. Don't be one of these people.

Even if it takes you a few minutes of feeling helpless and powerless before you reconnect to nature, that's ok. You're way ahead of most of the other people out there in the world.

The more that you notice when you are disconnecting yourself from nature, then the more you'll be able to bring yourself back into the connection until The Nature Process is such a part of your life that you don't have to think about it. You just follow Nike's example and "Do it."

Chapter 9: Be The Change

When I examine myself and my methods of thought I come to the conclusion that the gift of fantasy has meant more to me than my talent for absorbing positive knowledge.
- Albert Einstein

As you've been reading this book, I hope you're resolved to do the exercises and really experience the power of The Nature Process. It's one thing to know something intellectually but it's another thing to fully embody the knowledge. This takes your understanding to a whole new level and without it, The Nature Process is nothing more than an interesting tool that you're not picking up. There are already too many people speaking out about things that they truly don't understand. They have the information but not the knowledge. Don't be one of them. The future of humanity and the earth is too important for you not to do this.

As I've said before, I know that even with the knowledge that I have about The Nature Process, I'm still at the tip of the iceberg in terms of understanding what's possible through consciously connecting to nature. I also know that it's through this conscious connection that collectively we will be able to be the change we want to make in the world.

Planetary transformation starts with personal transformation. As you align yourself with nature's support you also align the world back into nature's support. Your perspective on the world changes and you see the truth of what needs to be done to create a world where peace, justice, and equality exists for all living beings. Most importantly, you then feel compelled to take action. Not because you feel obliged to, or because you fear what happens if you don't, but because it feels good to do so. You fully embody the knowledge that we are all one.

If you haven't, now is the time to go back and start doing the exercises outlined in this book. Doing them will bring you fully into your own natural power in a way that this book can't. Even as I read what I've written in this book I know that I can't even begin to capture with words the intensity and power of consciously connecting to nature. It's something that has to be experienced. This book is merely a tool that will help you to open your mind enough, to step beyond the educated ignorance that we live in and discover your own natural truth.

What you will get from The Nature Process will be similar but different to my experiences. We're all here to do our part in re-birthing the world. I can't tell you what your part is. But nature can. And when you ground yourself fully into nature you'll truly be able to make the change that you want to see in the world and do it in a way that is in alignment with nature's wisdom. There are already too many great ideas floating around in our world that have indirectly caused humanity to further disconnect from itself and from nature.

I've used quotes by Einstein throughout this book as he, for me, is the greatest thinker of the twentieth century. Yet even he was disconnected from nature. This was in spite of his love of nature, which is well documented. I once met someone who knew Einstein when she was a child (how cool is that?). He was a friend of the family of her best friend in childhood. Her memories of him were of a sweet, caring man who played the violin very well and kept turning up late because he's got lost in the gardens, literally smelling the flowers, on his way over.

His famous equation $E = MC^2$ (which I'm not going to even pretend to understand properly) was instrumental in the development of the atomic bomb, even though Einstein had nothing directly to do with its creation. Had he known, he would never have put his theory forward. Had he been fully connected to nature, he would have understood the full implications of his work and never released it to the world. Instead he would have destroyed it. Now this probably wouldn't have stopped atomic bombs being created but it might have delayed their production long enough so that they were never used as weapons of mass destruction within war. Just before his death, Einstein acknowledged that the greatest mistake of his life was signing a letter to President Roosevelt recommending that atomic bombs be made.

Even Hitler had a superficial love of nature, and we all know what he did. His fundamental disconnection from nature led to the deaths of at least 5.5 million Jews and millions of others victims because he couldn't understand and embody the truth inherent within nature that we are all one.

That's the power of a mind disconnected from nature.

Yet throughout history we have had people who have been truly connected to nature. Jesus (and Mary Magdalene, who supported Jesus in his work) was one of them. Jesus spent forty days and forty nights in the desert going through his own nature process. Over two thousand years later, his teachings are still relevant to the world. They were so revolutionary that people knew they'd never be able to destroy his legacy, so instead they chose to manipulate and twist it to their own ends. Despite that, the essential truth of his teachings remains for those who wish to discover it.

Buddha was another. He reached enlightenment after sitting under a tree going through his own nature process. He'd searched for years to end his suffering before that. In the four hundred years that it took before his teachings were committed to writing, the understanding of just how important the role of the tree was in this was lost. Yet again, despite his teachings being adapted by those who came afterwards, the power and essence of the insights he received from nature still remain influencing millions of people around the world.

That's the power of a mind connected to nature.

Our imagination is one of the most powerful tools that we have at our disposal. It's led to the world of magic that we now live in today. And it is magic. Imagine someone from a thousand years ago coming into our world and seeing what we're capable of. It's phenomenal, and it's directly down to the human imagination that has conceived the world we now live in. Humanity is capable of miracles. We've just forgotten to see the miracles for what they are. We've forgotten ourselves. Nature will remind us.

If you're truly serious about stepping up and consciously playing your part in bringing change to the world, whatever that part may be, then you need to plug yourself into nature. You need to go deeper than you've ever gone before. You need to see what's truly possible and let your imagination take flight. Grounded in nature, your imagination will soar to heights that previously you'd never have thought possible.

That's the power of nature.

This book contains everything you need to tap into the power of nature. Your own natural power is the power of nature. You are more powerful that you can possibly imagine. To step into and fully recognize that power all you need to do is get outside and start enhancing your natural presence. The more that you work on this, the deeper you'll go until you have a permanent natural presence that doesn't depend on you being physically connected to nature. You'll be able to access nature wherever you are.

I experienced this for the first time a few months ago as I was doing some further healing work in preparation for writing the latest book in the *Thriving* series, *Thriving Rape: Shift from Powerless to Powerful as You Heal Yourself and the Planet*. When I received the intuitive insight (while walking out in nature, of course) that I would write that book, I had thought that I had completely healed from my own rape. As I made the decision to go public about this I realized I still had healing to do, even after all the work I'd already done.

As I sat in a session with an awesome sexological bodyworker called Andrea Marlene (www.andreamarlenebodywork.com), she pointed out to me that it seemed as if behind my passion still lay anger, despite the work I'd already done to release it. As I sat with this I realized that I wasn't angry towards men *per se*, I was angry with the system of patriarchy that undermines both women and men. She challenged me to let go of my anger with a click of my fingers, which was something that I'd said to her about how easy it was to shift emotional baggage with nature.

We were inside at the time, no nature around. Then something flashed into my mind. A few months earlier, I had gotten a tattoo of two oak leaves and two acorns. Two days later I went to hang out with my friends, The Twins. These are two old lime trees near my mum's house set closely together. As I walked in a figure of eight symbol around the two trees, I felt my tattoo tingling. I didn't really think anymore of it. Until then. What if I could use the tattoo as an energetic representation of nature?

Inspired, right there in front of the bodyworker I talked myself through The Nature Process. Then with a click of my fingers I released decades' worth of hidden anger. Just like that I was no longer an angry eco-feminist. It was simple. Easy. Effortless. Magical. Since then I've used this technique again and again to ground myself into nature where it's not physically present and let go of emotional baggage and limiting beliefs when I've not been able to get outside.

To reach this point had taken me thirty years of nature processing, both unconscious and conscious. I didn't know what I was doing. But thanks to this book, you do. You'll be able to shave years off your journey if you want to.

The more you connect to your natural presence, the more you'll automatically start to experience your natural body. Nature outside will automatically connect with nature inside. You'll come to know your body intimately in a way you never thought possible. All the dogma about what our bodies are capable of will fade away. You'll experience your body in a way you can never see it. As you do, all the lies that the media pushes on us about what a "perfect" body should look like and the products needed to achieve this will fade from your mind. Your body is already perfect. Nature will help you believe that.

Due to the chronic ill health I've suffered from, I've always been conscious of my body. When you're in so much pain, it's hard not to be. Asthma and eczema have challenged me my whole life. At times they've severely limited what my body is capable of doing, and nearly killed me a few times.

As a result I learned to view my body as weak. Something that was reinforced by western medicine. I had to be careful of what I did with it. If the weather was cold and damp I couldn't go outside. It might make me ill. If I did too much exercise it'd trigger my asthma and eczema. So I stopped exercising. I despised my body for this perceived weakness. I used food as a tool of punishment against it. The guilt and shame that came along with this paralyzed me for years before I finally turned to nature for support.

The last flare-up I had of my eczema was five years ago. As I mentioned in chapter one, eighty-five percent of my body was covered with red, itchy, inflamed skin. I sought advice from the leading dermatologist in Spain. His advice made my skin worse. When he told me to get out of the way and let him treat me, I left and never went back. Instead I started listening to my body and letting it tell me what it needed to do to heal. My body was so badly out of balance that it took years to work through the underlying causes of my eczema and rebalance my body but I did it.

Now I'm doing the same with my asthma. Before my eczema flare-up I hardly ever needed inhalers. On the odd occasion that my asthma did flare up, I could breathe through it without medication. I lost that, along with my confidence to do so, the more that the side effects of eczema took my body out of balance. Recently I did some breath work to help me manage it better. During a session I realized just how much I'd hated my lungs for not working properly. There was deep sadness around this to be released. Now I realize just how powerful they are. I've tortured them with mindless smoking, disrespected them with bad food choices, put them in toxic environments, and still they've fought to keep me alive. Wow.

Today I see my body as a miracle. I'm in awe of just how powerful it is. For the first time in my life I'm attracted to caring for my body as if it were a temple and to see just how magnificent it can be if I truly take care of it. It may have taken me thirty-four years to reach this understanding, but I have the rest of my life to put it into practice.

The power of your natural presence and your natural body together will make it easier for you to follow your natural attractions. Doing what feels good will become more important than duty, obligation and enforced responsibility. It will become your default behavior, not just within The Nature Process but also within your life.

Now I don't mean this in terms of some of the irresponsible hippy bullshit that came out of the counter-culture revolution in the sixties and seventies. Following your natural attractions in their essential purity means a deep awareness of how your actions affect others. After all, they are merely a reflection of yourself. If you hurt them, you hurt yourself.

When I arrived in Ibiza in January 2014, I was attracted to leaving my bedroom doors open. All the time. This mean that in winter I needed a good few layers to keep me warm as the chill of winter entered my room. Yet this was an invitation for nature to come into my room and into me in a way that I'd never allowed before. Only as I write this do I realize just how fundamental this shift was for me in light of the beliefs I had around my asthma as I shared above.

One of my landlady's cats, Hindu, who supported me during my natural release, started to keep me company. Normally this shy cat would hide at the bottom of the garden and never come in the house. But soon, I couldn't get rid of her! Before long I had not only all four of my landlady's cats entering my bedroom but also some of the local strays seeking food and water. Cats have been a key part of my life since I was a child. I feel incomplete without one.

Then one of the cats, a lovely ginger tom, who you also met during my natural release, started bringing ticks into my room. I'd find them crawling across the bed or on the floor. Yes, my initial reaction was the same as yours. Then I realized I had an opportunity to work with the energy of the ticks. What did they mean? What could I learn from them? As soon I got this, they stopped coming into my room.

Lizards and geckos entered my room and I learned from them. Mice entered my room and I learned from them. Bird song was my constant companion. As the weather got warmer, mosquitoes entered my room. As much as I learned from them, I also ended up killing as many as possible after they kept on biting me! There's still work to be done there.

This was an intense learning experience for me that took me even deeper into my connection with nature. Yet none of it would have been possible if I hadn't followed my own natural attraction to keeping my outside bedroom door open.

As you can see from the above story, following your natural attraction gives you many opportunities to develop your natural communication with nature in all its forms. You'll get chances to interact with the planet you live in and with your non-human siblings that you'd never get to otherwise.

I've always been more connected to trees and the earth. This communication comes naturally to me. Animals, on the other hand, have been more challenging. Coryelle, the animal communicator, told me that for most people it was the other way around.

I'd left Ibiza to visit family in Scotland and attend a conference in England. Upon my return, there was a stray cat that had appeared around the house while I'd been away. When I opened my bedroom doors, the cat shot into my room and didn't leave.

Yet her behavior was strange. She was really aggressive towards the other cats and a couple of times she'd peed on my bed. Gross. I've had many cats throughout my life, yet her behavior was like nothing I'd ever seen. I felt so sorry for her, and thought that she must have gone through something so traumatic to act like this.

I arranged an appointment with Coryelle. What she told me blew my mind. I'd been interpreting the cat's behavior through the lens of being human. When she started explaining what *she* was picking up from the cat, I started laughing. I'd totally misunderstood this cat's behavior. I'd made the mistake of interpreting the cat's behavior through my human lens. She wasn't traumatized. She was making sure that I paid attention to her and that the other cats weren't distracting me. She conveyed her dislike of the name I'd given her and, through Coryelle, explained that she'd come to help me with my work.

Within twenty-four hours of speaking with Coryelle, the cat's attitude had totally changed. More powerfully though, is that I then became capable of communicating with this cat after Coryelle taught me a few tricks. This took my natural communication to a whole new level.

Nin, as the cat likes to be called, taught me so much over the next five weeks. It was also the five weeks that The Nature Process first ran. Nin was there supporting me and even took part in The Nature Process, which was commented on by one of the participants when she appeared in one of the sessions staring directly into the camera.

The more you practice The Nature Process, the more powerful your natural releases will become. You'll be able to shift limiting beliefs and energetic blockages yourself that before you'd need additional support and guidance with.

Recently I had the opportunity to try *ayahuasca* for the first time, which is a plant medicine from the Amazon known for creating altered states of consciousness that promote healing. I had a powerful experience with the plant, yet the altered state of consciousness was exactly the same as what I experience through my conscious connection to nature. In fact, my conscious connection to nature is more powerful because it's softer and gentler in its approach and I can use it any time I want without the nasty purging effects of *ayahuasca*.

Once you reach this stage with The Nature Process you can tie your natural release into other aspects of nature. At the last new moon I had an urge to dance and dance wildly. I put music on my MP3 player that I hadn't listened to for ages. I went outside to the garden in my bare feet and danced under the darkness of the sky filled with shining stars. Sweat coated my body as the balmy wind danced against my skin. That was natural presence and natural body supported by the music and dance.

Staring up at the sky I was attracted to one star shining in the sky. It was no brighter than any other, and as I expanded my view I realized it was part of the constellation Libra, which is significant for me. Not only am I a Libran but I have the star constellation tattooed on my skin. This was my natural attraction.

I connected with the star using my natural communication. It twinkled and seemed to pulsate with a brighter energy for a second. Sensing that as consent, I continued to dance with my awareness focused fully on the star. As I did I sensed myself in that star. I became conscious of myself with my feet on the ground at the same time that I shone down up myself.

The next few hours were transformative for me. In all honesty I have no idea what I released. I went back to my room and lay down with candles and incense burning. My whole body was shaking. A name popped into my head, Arcadia, and I was attracted to searching for information on it. You won't be surprised to find out that the name was connected to the Golden Age of Men, a period of primordial peace and prosperity, when humanity was still fully connected to nature. This information caused the sensations to intensify within my body.

I had to go and lie down on the earth outside. I burped and stretched my body as even more energy was released. It was enjoyable even with the intensity of the experience.

When I returned to my bed again and lay down I got a flash of insight into what my next tattoo would be. Now before you think that this was an impulsive action, the tattoo was something that I'd been contemplating for years but it had never felt right. There was something missing in the symbolism of it.

Next day I received an email from my tattoo artist telling me he was moving studios. I told him what I wanted, and when I returned to Scotland I got it done. Each tattoo I get is consciously chosen for the meaning behind it. This is without a doubt the most powerful tattoo I've ever had with the layers of depth and meaning incorporated into it.

I tattooed the name associated with the Golden Age of Men on my right lower arm in the Elder Futhark runes. This is the oldest form of the runic alphabets and they were also used for divination and magic. Not only do I have the name but I also have the combined power of the meaning of each of these runes. It's not a pretty tattoo. In fact, I've been told it looks like I've drawn on my arm with felt pen. That's what makes it truly beautiful to me. I love knowing that very few people understand the symbolism and significance of it.

Now I'm not advocating tattoos here as part of your natural process. This is my personal way of integrating my natural power. It doesn't have to be yours.

Once you understand the principles of The Nature Process, you'll be able to play with them and adapt the process to you personally just like I have. That's where the fun really starts. You'll find that it connects to many other experiences you've had, along with other things you're interested in. For example, if you're into yoga, then how do you incorporate that into The Nature Process? What about running? Or diving? Or writing? Or making music? Or having fun with your friends? The possibilities are endless. The only limits are the limits of your imagination.

Take this process and make it your own. When you do, I want to hear about it. Nothing excites me more. Reach out and email me at tabitha@tabithajayne.com. When you share your experience with me I can share it with others. We need many different voices speaking up about their experiences. There are some people who won't be able to hear what I'm sharing, but they'll be able to hear it when *you* share it. You can become the inspiration that encourages even more people to get outside and get consciously connected to nature.

If you want to become part of The Nature Process community, then consider going through the program live the next time it runs. There's power in sharing your experience with others, being supported as you develop, deepening your own nature process, and contributing to the collective energy of a group of people all consciously connecting to nature at the same time. The additional benefit of this is that you'll also be giving directly back to the earth. You'll find more information about this at www.thenatureprocessonline.com.

For a long time I've hidden the insights I've received from nature deep inside. I first started nature processing when I was around five years old. I didn't know what I was doing at the time; all I knew is that when I tried to explain or talk about this, people didn't understand. The fact that people are now interested and able to grasp what I'm talking about is actually quite bemusing to me. All my life I've judged and ridiculed myself for the beliefs and experiences I've had, yet now I find that they are more valuable than I ever knew. I thought I was the weird one, that there was something wrong with me. Yet what I've known my whole life is what people have been trying to discover for years. Who would have thought?

When I first came across the world of personal growth, I felt insecure. People were talking about the latest book or course that had helped them discover more of themselves and how wonderful these teachers were. I had no idea what they were talking about. Yet when I started reading the books and doing the courses I found that I'd already outgrown a lot of the stuff they were teaching. Nature had given me the same insights years ago while I'd been outside going for a walk or climbing a tree.

This is my truth as discovered through my own fifty-four senses. Even as I sit here typing this, I'm aware of nature on a whole new level. To sit here typing knowing on an embodied level that I am nothing more than energy and vibrating space that reaches out through everything in the universe is pretty mind-blowing. I keep stopping to stare at my hands. Although I stare at them with my eyes and they look the same, on a sensory level they are completely different.

I am nature simultaneously present in the concept of the self known as Tabi but also in each and every living thing on this planet. Holy shit! There are no words that adequately describe what I'm experiencing to you, and what you can experience for yourself.

I stare around my mum's living room observing the mundane nature of the room yet sensing that this is nothing more than an extension of me. I look at the Rowan tree outside the window, watch it dance in the wind, and feel the wind on my skin at the same time.

It's like being on the biggest psychedelic trip of my life. Yet there's no drugs involved. Only nature. Moreover, I can access this state at will with very little effort.

I've lived in this world for so long that I'd forgotten just how extraordinary it is and how easy it is to access it at will. When I was creating The Nature Process Online a friend came out to visit me in Ibiza. I'd been trying to explain the power of nature to her for weeks. Now she's one of the most spiritually aware people I've met, yet I couldn't get this concept across to her. That night we were sitting out in the garden under the full moon after a walk down to a lovely little beach with another friend. All of a sudden she starts shaking and looking around like she's lost her freaking mind.

I could feel the energy shifting in her and rising up. I started telling her about nature. And finally she got what I'd been trying to communicate to her for weeks. It was an awesome moment for me (and her!). As she described what she was experiencing for the first time, I finally got to see just how totally cool this is. For someone else to get the world that I live in on such a cellular level...wow!

She said to me afterwards that I really needed to talk about nature in a deep voice, calling it "NAAAAAAATTTUUUUUURE," so that people could really feel its power and scope.

It's the total embodiment of everything we've been told is impossible, then charged by nature, so that we can finally feel the truth. We are nature. We are one. Our minds, grounded in nature, are the most powerful tools we have at our disposal. We are our own free energy source and can literally move mountains with our minds, if only we let go of the limiting beliefs that hold us back from doing so. We have the ability to re-birth the world in a myriad of magical ways that we've only previously read, thought about, and consigned to fiction.

I don't want you to take my word for it. I want you to get out into nature and experience this for yourself. If you've made it this far in the book, you already have a connection to nature. It might be strong. It might be weak. It doesn't matter. You start where you are. The only place you can go is deeper. Everyone's journey is their own. There is no right or wrong way. There is only the way. Trust in nature and it will lead you where you need to go.

At the start of the book I asked you whether you wanted to take the red pill or the blue pill. By continuing to read—and hopefully act—you chose the red one. This is the truth that you've been waiting to hear. Now it's time to experience it. You're already in Wonderland and it's time to let nature show you just how deep the rabbit hole goes. In all honesty, I can't tell you about the power of The Nature Process, no matter how much I try. Words are inadequate. You have to sense it for yourself. That's why it's so important that you go back to the exercises I've laid out in this book again and again.

In the film *The Matrix*, after Neo takes the red pill and wakes up, he asks Morpheus why his eyes hurt. Morpheus replies that it's because he's never used them before. It's same with your senses. Your fifty-four senses have been deadened from the moment you were born. You probably didn't even know of their existence until you read this book. That's how persuasive the myth of the five senses is. That's how distorted our beliefs are. Everything you've been told is a lie. It's up to you to find the truth.

Just like Neo, you're on a mission to believe. To believe in nature. To believe in yourself. To believe in the impossible. You've spent your entire life looking for something that's been right in front of you the whole time. The earth is a physical manifestation of the power of nature that you don't need faith to believe in. It's here right in front of you. All you need to do is open your mind, see with your heart and let go of every single false belief that's been pumped into your head since you were born. Step up into your natural power. Once you start to do this you don't need to hope that humanity and the earth can be saved; you'll know with every fiber of your being that they can.

You know the path you need to take with The Nature Process. Now it's time to walk it. When you do, you'll discover that you're able to free your mind from all fear, doubt and disbelief. You'll be able to see beyond the obstacles that keep you trapped in a state of pretend powerlessness, and step fully into your natural power.

Then you'll wake up to the biggest truth of them all. This is most important game you'll ever play. It's called life.

Once you realize this fundamental truth, you'll find you can't help but share your experience with others. You know that what's on the other side of fear, doubt, and disbelief is so much better than where most people are. The more people we have to show others the door to humanity's natural power, the easier it is for them to walk through it and join us on the other side.

Nature is the key and I've just given it to you.

Remember, together we're changing the world. Together, we will create a world that is whole and balanced.

As part of my commitment to help you integrate The Nature Process into your daily life I hold three Q&A webinars a year where you can ask questions and gain further support with The Nature Process.

If you bought this book through one of The Nature Process Retreats or ordered it directly from my website the email address you provided at the time will be automatically added to receive notifications about these webinars.

However, if you bought this book from another source you will need to email tabithajayne@tabithajayne.com to request that you receive access to the Q&A webinars.

I hope to meet you virtually during one of the webinars!

Additional Resources

If you've enjoyed The Nature Process and would like to bring it to life in your community, organization or business the following resources are for you.

The Nature Process Workshops/Retreats

These custom designed workshops are tailored to your specific needs and enable your community or organization to experience the power of The Nature Process in person and outside. Following The Nature Process, participants are guided individually to free themselves from the past and discover how they would like to be the change they want to make in the world. These workshops can be facilitated by Tabi or by one of The Nature Process facilitators.

Email: tabithajayne@tabithajayne.com for more information.

The Nature Process Presentations

Tabi offers a powerful, dynamic and inspirational presentation based around The Nature Process, "Step into your natural power and be the change you want to make in the world" that can be specifically adapted to your audience. The Nature Process can also be specifically adapted to your needs to ensure a memorable and engaging presentation for your audience. You can find Tabi's media kit at: www.tabithajayne.com/about/the-nature-process-media-kit

The Nature Process Facilitator Training

This training is specifically designed for those who wish to support others through The Nature Process either in-person or online. You'll be personally guided through The Nature Process before then working through the online training resources that show you how to explain, teach, facilitate and integrate The Nature Process into your life and business. You'll also receive live training calls with Tabitha Jayne and receive ongoing support via the online facilitator community.

Email tabitha@tabithajayne.com for more information.

The Nature Process Affiliate Scheme

As part of Tabi's commitment to planet first, not profit and creating a win-win-win result for all involved you also have the opportunity to sign up as an affiliate and be paid to spread the word about The Nature Process book.

For every copy of the book you sell you can received approximately $5 commission. To find out more about this opportunity go to: www.tabithajayne.com/affiliates

About Tabi(tha) Jayne

Tabi(tha) Jayne is a business growth consultant, author, speaker, coach and ecopsychologist who is passionate about helping people and organizations transform themselves with the healing power of nature.

In 2013 she received her Master's in Applied Ecopsychology from Akamai University, Hawaii in collaboration with the Institute of Global Education/Project NatureConnect. She is also a Certified Professional Coach with the International Coach Academy.

Tabi is the author of Thriving Loss: Move beyond grief to a place of peace, passion and purpose and the creator of the Tree of Transformation®, which helps professionals and organizations to eliminate stress and cultivate productivity, creativity and innovation to increase well-being, work more effectively and maximize profits.

In 2014, Tabi was awarded The Xtraordinary Lady's Star Award for her work around helping people to free themselves from their past.

Tabi's journey started after the sudden death of her younger brother, Peter in a car crash in 2002. Following this, Tabi set up and ran a Scottish charity aimed at helping young adults affected by bereavement. During this time she was a finalist in the UK Everywoman 2004 Artemis awards as well as Cosmopolitan's Fun, Fearless, Female Awards 2006. The charity was also featured in the Channel 4 documentary for schools, 'Without You'.

You can find out more about Tabi at www.tabithajayne.com

Acknowledgements

This book wouldn't have been possible without the work of Dr. Michael J. Cohen. His work has provided me with the roots of understanding exactly what happens to us when we're out in nature and allowed me to develop my understanding of how nature works further.

I'd also like to thank Betty Hames, fellow Master in Applied Ecopsychology for her support and belief in me as I not only launched The Nature Process LIVE Online but also wrote this book.

My editor, Thomas Hauck has helped polish my writing so that it sparkles and shines. I'm truly grateful for his speedy and professional work!

Also, I'd grateful to Ashish Joshi for his awesome work in designing the cover of the book. He's truly the best graphic designer anyone could wish for.

Thanks to Carly Hope, for challenging me to create The Nature Process LIVE Online; Melody Fletcher, who was my guinea pig and sounding board; and Clare Dakin and Edveeje Fairchild from TreeSisters, whose support and belief in me and my work was invaluable.

Special thanks goes to the land in Ibiza, France and Andorra. This book wouldn't have been possible without the connection and inspiration I received from it.

Last but not least, thank you to every person who signed up for The Nature Process LIVE Online in May 2014, especially Sami Aaron. Their questions and feedback helped shape this book and make it even better. I'm honored to have had the chance to share nature with them in this way. This is not just my book. It's theirs too.

Pay It Forward

Through my lifetime partnership with the non-profit Buy1Give1 (B1G1) I'm excited to share that every copy sold of this book supports the adoption of ten trees at Khai Yai National Park in Thailand for a year.

A tree nursery and planting project has been established there to aid in the fight against deforestation and climate change. The project aims to replace the lost forest while building on the community's awareness and knowledge of sustainable agriculture.

Your purchase of this book, either in print or electronically, helps to ensure the survival of flora and fauna along with the restoration of a healthy environment.

On behalf of the trees, thank you!

If you'd like to find out more information about B1G1 go to www.b1g1.com and if you decide to register with them too please use the code **nature** for an additional surprise.

Made in the USA
San Bernardino, CA
01 March 2016